THE DOCTOR WHO
PROGRAMME GUIDE

Volume 2

THE DOCTOR WHO PROGRAMME GUIDE

Volume 2

Jean-Marc Lofficier

A TARGET BOOK
published by
the Paperback Division of
W.H. ALLEN & CO. LTD

A Target Book
Published in 1981
By the Paperback Division of
W.H. Allen & Co. Ltd
A Howard & Wyndham Company
44 Hill Street, London W1X 8LB

Typeset by Phoenix Photosetting, Chatham
Printed and bound in Great Britain

ISBN 0 426 20142 6

This book gives details of *Doctor Who* programmes
televised by the BBC up to the time of going to press.

ACKNOWLEDGEMENTS

I am deeply grateful to the following people who helped me in the compilation of the information included in this book: Jeremy Bentham, Christopher H. Bidmead, Eric Hoffman, David Howe, Barry Letts, Ian Levine, John McElroy, John Nathan-Turner, John Peel, Graham Williams, the BBC *Doctor Who* Production Office and the members of the *Doctor Who* Appreciation Society.

Special thanks are particularly due to Terrance Dicks, whose help and advice were invaluable in the making of this book.

J.-M.L.

To my wife, Randy

CONTENTS

FOREWORD

When a BBC Producer is a 142 years old (or does it just feel like that?), he regenerates and turns into an Executive Producer, or so they say; and then people from all over the world write and ask him questions; and he gets the answers wrong . . .

Well, perhaps I don't get them all wrong, but to be corrected by a 15-year-old about the third monster on the left in a show made before he was born can be an earth-shaking experience.

But now, thanks to the quite extraordinary industry of Jean-Marc Lofficier, I can be right every time. And so can you—and you—and you. Though you, sir, who pointed out that in various *Doctor Who* stories there have been three entirely different and incompatible versions of the destruction of Atlantis, presumably won't need the help of Jean-Marc.

Of course, he hasn't been able to put everything down; his self-imposed brief couldn't allow it even if he could have persuaded the publishers to accept a manuscript the length of the *Encyclopaedia Britannica*. In any case, a lot of it's secret.

For example, it will always remain untold that one of the monsters in an early Jon Pertwee story was familiarly known to one and all as Puff the Magic Dragon, looking as he did like an 8-foot-long pink-quilted pyjama case.

My lips will be even more firmly sealed about the various suggestions put forward concerning the inter-personal relationships of Alpha Centauri, the hermaphrodite hexapod. After all, even snails must have a surprisingly interesting social life and they don't have six arms.

Anything short of such revelations (which will only be made known 300 years after the Doctor's last regeneration) is sure to be found in this remarkable work of eccentric but dedicated scholarship.

Barry Letts

TABLE OF STORIES

The title of each serial is preceded by its story production code.

First Doctor (1963–1966)

First Season

A   An Unearthly Child (4 episodes)
        (Episodes 2, 3 and 4 are also collectively known
        as The Tribe of Gum, but An Unearthly Child is
        the correct BBC designation for all four
        episodes.)
B   The Daleks (7 episodes)
C   The Edge of Destruction (2 episodes)
        (Often wrongly referred to as Beyond the Sun)
D   Marco Polo (7 episodes)
E   The Keys of Marinus (6 episodes)
F   The Aztecs (6 episodes)
G   The Sensorites (6 episodes)
H   The Reign of Terror (6 episodes)

Second Season

J   Planet of Giants (3 episodes)
K   The Dalek Invasion of Earth (6 episodes)
L   The Rescue (2 episodes)
M   The Romans (4 episodes)
N   The Web Planet (6 episodes)
P   The Crusade (4 episodes)
Q   The Space Museum (4 episodes)
R   The Chase (6 episodes)
S   The Time Meddler (4 episodes)

Third Season

T   Galaxy Four (4 episodes)
T/A   Mission to the Unknown (1 episode)
U   The Myth Makers (4 episodes)
V   The Dalek Masterplan (12 episodes)
W   The Massacre (4 episodes)
Y   The Ark (4 episodes)
X   The Celestial Toymaker (4 episodes)
Z   The Gunfighters (4 episodes)
AA   The Savages (4 episodes)
BB   The War Machines (4 episodes)

Fourth Season

CC   The Smugglers (4 episodes)
DD   The Tenth Planet (4 episodes)

Second Doctor (1966–1969)

Fourth Season (continued)

EE   The Power of the Daleks (6 episodes)
FF   The Highlanders (4 episodes)
GG   The Underwater Menace (4 episodes)
HH   The Moonbase (4 episodes)
JJ   The Macra Terror (4 episodes)
KK   The Faceless Ones (6 episodes)
LL   The Evil of the Daleks (7 episodes)

Fifth Season

MM   The Tomb of the Cybermen (4 episodes)
NN   The Abominable Snowmen (6 episodes)
OO   The Ice Warriors (6 episodes)
PP   The Enemy of the World (6 episodes)
QQ   The Web of Fear (6 episodes)
RR   Fury from the Deep (6 episodes)
SS   The Wheel in Space (6 episodes)

Sixth Season

TT   The Dominators (5 episodes)
UU   The Mind Robber (5 episodes)
VV   The Invasion (8 episodes)
WW   The Krotons (4 episodes)
XX   The Seeds of Death (6 episodes)
YY   The Space Pirates (6 episodes)
ZZ   The War Games (10 episodes)

Third Doctor (1970–1974)

Seventh Season

AAA   Spearhead from Space (4 episodes)
BBB   The Silurians (7 episodes)
CCC   The Ambassadors of Death (7 episodes)
DDD Inferno (7 episodes)

Eighth Season

EEE   Terror of the Autons (4 episodes)
FFF   The Mind of Evil (6 episodes)
GGG The Claws of Axos (4 episodes)
HHH Colony in Space (6 episodes)
JJJ   The Daemons (5 episodes)

Ninth Season

KKK Day of the Daleks (4 episodes)
MMM The Curse of Peladon (4 episodes)
LLL   The Sea Devils (6 episodes)
NNN The Mutants (6 episodes)
OOO The Time Monster (6 episodes)

Tenth Season

RRR The Three Doctors (4 episodes)
PPP   Carnival of Monsters (4 episodes)
QQQ Frontier in Space (6 episodes)
SSS   Planet of the Daleks (6 episodes)
TTT   The Green Death (6 episodes)

Eleventh Season

UUU The Time Warrior (4 episodes)

WWW Invasion of the Dinosaurs (6 episodes)
XXX Death to the Daleks (4 episodes)
YYY The Monster of Peladon (6 episodes)
ZZZ Planet of the Spiders (6 episodes)

Fourth Doctor (1974–1981)

Twelfth Season

4A   Robot (4 episodes)
4C   The Ark in Space (4 episodes)
4B   The Sontaran Experiment (2 episodes)
4E   Genesis of the Daleks (6 episodes)
4D   Revenge of the Cybermen (4 episodes)

Thirteenth Season

4F   Terror of the Zygons (4 episodes)
4H   Planet of Evil (4 episodes)
4G   Pyramids of Mars (4 episodes)
4J   The Android Invasion (4 episodes)
4K   The Brain of Morbius (4 episodes)
4L   The Seeds of Doom (6 episodes)

Fourteenth Season

4M   The Masque of Mandragora (4 episodes)
4N   The Hand of Fear (4 episodes)
4P   The Deadly Assassin (4 episodes)
4Q   The Face of Evil (4 episodes)
4R   The Robots of Death (4 episodes)
4S   The Talons of Weng-Chiang (6 episodes)

Fifteenth Season

4V   Horror of Fang Rock (4 episodes)

4T	The Invisible Enemy (4 episodes)
4X	Image of the Fendahl (4 episodes)
4W	The Sunmakers (4 episodes)
4Y	Underworld (4 episodes)
4Z	The Invasion of Time (6 episodes)

Sixteenth Season

5A	The Ribos Operation (4 episodes)
5B	The Pirate Planet (4 episodes)
5C	The Stones of Blood (4 episodes)
5D	The Androids of Tara (4 episodes)
5E	The Power of Kroll (4 episodes)
5F	The Armageddon Factor (6 episodes)

Seventeenth Season

5J	Destiny of the Daleks (4 episodes)
5H	City of Death (4 episodes)
5G	The Creature from the Pit (4 episodes)
5K	Nightmare of Eden (4 episodes)
5L	The Horns of Nimon (4 episodes)
5M	Shada (6 episodes)

Eighteenth Season

5N	The Leisure Hive (4 episodes)
5Q	Meglos (4 episodes)
5R	Full Circle (4 episodes)
5P	State of Decay (4 episodes)
5S	Warriors' Gate (4 episodes)
5T	The Keeper of Traken (4 episodes)
5V	Logopolis (4 episodes)

INDICES

Stories are referred to by their production codes.
See Table of Stories for key to code.

2

1 The Doctor's Companions

FIRST DOCTOR (WILLIAM HARTNELL)

Susan Foreman, the Doctor's granddaughter (Carole Ann Ford): A–K
Ian Chesterton (William Russell): A–R
Barbara Wright (Jacqueline Hill): A–R
Vicki (Maureen O'Brien): L–U
Steven Taylor (Peter Purves): R–AA
Katarina (Adrienne Hill): U–V
Sara Kingdom (Jean Marsh): V
Dodo Chaplet (Jackie Lane): W–BB
Ben Jackson (Michael Craze): BB–DD (*continued*)
Polly (Anneke Willis): BB–DD (*continued*)

SECOND DOCTOR (PATRICK TROUGHTON)

Ben Jackson (Michael Craze): EE–KK
Polly (Anneke Willis): EE–KK
Jamie McCrimmon (Frazer Hines): FF–ZZ
Victoria Waterfield (Deborah Watling): LL–RR
Zoe (Wendy Padbury): SS–ZZ
Brigadier Lethbridge-Stewart (Nicholas Courtney): QQ, VV
Benton (John Levene): VV

THIRD DOCTOR (JON PERTWEE)

Liz Shaw (Caroline John): AAA–DDD
Jo Grant (Katy Manning): EEE–TTT

Brigadier Lethbridge-Stewart (Nicholas Courtney): AAA–DDD, EEE–JJJ, KKK, OOO, RRR, TTT, UUU, WWW, ZZZ
Benton (John Levene): CCC–GGG, JJJ, KKK, OOO, RRR, TTT, WWW, ZZZ
Captain Yates (Richard Franklin): EEE–GGG, JJJ, KKK, OOO, TTT, WWW, ZZZ
Master (Roger Delgado): EEE–JJJ, LLL, OOO, QQQ
Sarah Jane Smith (Elizabeth Sladen): UUU–ZZZ (*continued*)

FOURTH DOCTOR (TOM BAKER)

Sarah Jane Smith (Elizabeth Sladen): 4A–4N
Harry Sullivan (Ian Marter): 4A–4F, 4J
Brigadier Lethbridge-Stewart (Nicholas Courtney): 4A, 4F
Benton (John Levene): 4A, 4F, 4J
Leela (Louise Jameson): 4Q–4Z
K9 (John Leeson): 4T–5F, 5N–5S; (David Brierley): 5G–5M
Lady Romanadvoratrelundar (Mary Tamm); 5A–5F; (Lalla Ward): 5J–5S
Adric (Matthew Waterhouse): 5R–5V
Nyssa (Sarah Sutton): 5T, 5V
Tegan Jovanka (Janet Fielding): 5V

2 What's What on *Who*

Capitalised words appear as separate entries.

Abbot of Amboise: Double of the First Doctor.
Encountered before the ST BARTHOLOMEW'S
DAY MASSACRE (W).

Achilles: Greek hero from the TROJAN WAR (U).

Adrasta (Lady): Ruler of CHLORIS, a green planet
without metals which she ruled with the help of her
HUNTSMAN. She had a monopoly of metal on the
planet, and was killed by ERATO (5G).

Adric: One of the Doctor's companions. This young,
mathematically gifted Alzarian boy stowed away in the
TARDIS (5R–5V).

Aggedor: Mythical beast protecting the planet
PELADON and its kings. Very real monster
encountered by the Third Doctor, who was able to
mesmerise it. Misused twice by evil parties, Aggedor
was finally killed by the human traitor, ECKERSLEY
(MMM, YYY).

Alpha Centauri: Name given to the six-armed being
from the planet of the same name. He acted as
Ambassador of the FEDERATION to PELADON and
befriended the Third Doctor (MMM, YYY).

Altos: Accompanied the First Doctor on his quest for
the KEYS OF MARINUS. He married Sabetha,
daughter of ARBITAN (E).

Alydon: Thal leader on Skaro (B).

Alzarius: Planet located in E-space where a starliner
from Earth crashed. It is inhabited by marsh creatures
who later evolved into Humans (5R).

Amdo: Goddess of the fishmen from Atlantis (GG).

Amplified Panatropic Compiler (APC Net): Giant
computer containing all the memories of all the TIME
LORDS who ever lived (4P, 4Z).

Andor: Leader of the SEVATEEM. He was killed by XOANON (4Q).

Andred: Commander of the Chancellery Guards from GALLIFREY. He married LEELA after the Sontaran invasion (4Z).

Androids: see ROBOTS.

Aneth: Planet that paid a tribute of youth and radioactive crystals to SKONNOS (5L).

Animus: Spider-like entity which controlled the ZARBI. It was destroyed by an isotope operated by BARBARA WRIGHT (N).

Antarctic: Principally the location of a South Pole base attacked by the CYBERMEN in the late 1980s (DD). Also the location of two buried Krynoid pods (4L).

Anti-matter: Always trouble! (RRR, 4H).

Antiquity: Period of EARTH HISTORY frequently visited by the Doctor (including but not limited to the following stories: M, U, V).

Arak: Leader of the Human revolt against the Spiders on Metebelis 3 (ZZZ).

Arbitan: Keeper of the CONSCIENCE of MARINUS. He was killed by the VOORDS (E).

Arcturus: Ambassador of the planet of the same name to PELADON. Prisoner of his tank-like life-support system, he was the villain of the story (MMM).

Argolis: Location of the LEISURE HIVE. Argolis was almost totally destroyed in a nuclear war with the FOAMASI. The Argolin were a dying race until their leader, MENA, found a method of rejuvenation in Tachyonics (5N).

Aridius: Desert-like but inhabited planet. The First Doctor stopped there while being pursued by the DALEKS. It was peopled by half-humanoid, half-amphibian creatures, the Aridians, and their enemies, the Mire Beasts (R).

Arnold (Sergeant): Colonel Lethbridge-Stewart's Aide during the YETI invasion. His mind was controlled by the GREAT INTELLIGENCE (QQ).

Ark: (1) Space Ark encountered by the First Doctor. Fleeing the imminent destruction of Earth, it was travelling to the planet REFUSIS. It was peopled by Humans and their servitors, the MONOIDS. A cold germ introduced by DODO made the Monoids stronger than the Humans (Y).

(2) Name given to space station NERVA, converted into an Ark in the 29th century to preserve the best specimens of Mankind from solar flares. It was invaded by the WIRRN (4C, 4B).

Ashe: A Colonist on the planet EXARIUS (HHH).

Astra (Princess): Princess of ATRIOS. In reality the sixth segment of the KEY TO TIME. When ROMANA regenerated, she adopted Astra's likeness (5F).

Astrid: Assistant to Giles KENT. She rescued the Second Doctor on an Australian beach (PP).

Atlantis: The Island of Atlantis was ruled by King DALLIOS. After the betrayal of Queen GALLEIA, it was destroyed by KRONOS and the MASTER (OOO). Also said to have been destroyed by AZAL, the Daemon (JJJ). Some survivors might have become the fishmen exploited by Professor ZAROFF (GG).

Atrios: Twin planet of ZEOS, Atrios was the Doctor's last stop in his quest for the KEY TO TIME. Atrios was nearly destroyed in a nuclear war arranged by the SHADOW (5F).

Aukon: Formerly known as Science Officer O'Connor of the Earth ship *Hydrax*. Drawn into E-SPACE by the GREAT VAMPIRE, Aukon became one of the immortal vampire rulers of a local planet (along with his colleagues ZARGO and CAMILLA). He died when the Doctor destroyed the Great Vampire (5P).

Australia: Visited by the Second Doctor when he saved the world from the threat of SALAMANDER (PP).

Autloc: Aztec High Priest of Knowledge (F).

Autons: Plastic mannikins controlled by the Nestene. A ray-gun is hidden in their wrists (AAA, EEE).

Axos: Single entity which is both ship and passengers simultaneously. It can look like beautiful golden beings or like a crawling mass of tentacles. With the help of a substance which is part of itself—Axonite—it steals the energy of hapless worlds. Axos allied itself with the MASTER to destroy Earth. It was time-looped by the Third Doctor (GGG).

Azal: Last of the DAEMONS. He was found at DEVIL'S END by the MASTER. Azal normally existed at a microscopic level but could reach gigantic proportions and had a god-like power. He offered to bestow it to the Doctor, who refused. He was defeated by his own energy, deflected by Jo GRANT who interposed herself between the Daemon and the Doctor (JJJ).

Azaxyr: Leader of the ICE WARRIORS on PELADON. Agent of GALAXY 5, he betrayed the FEDERATION in his desire for glory. He was killed by GEBEK (YYY).

Aztecs: Encountered by the First Doctor in (F).

Azure: Planet that was the destination of the spaceship *Empress* which crashed into the *Hecate* while in HYPERSPACE (5K).

Barnham: Convict at STANGMOOR Prison. He helped the Third Doctor to defeat the MASTER and the MIND PARASITE (FFF).

Bellal: One of the more advanced EXXILON, and a friend of the Third Doctor (XXX).

Bennett: Murderer. Posing as a Didonian creature, KOQUILION, he befriended VICKI (L).

Benoit: A scientist on the Moonbase (HH).

Benton: Corporal, Sergeant, then RSM of UNIT. A loyal man (VV, CCC, DDD, EEE, FFF, GGG, JJJ, KKK, OOO, RRR, TTT, WWW, ZZZ, 4A, 4F, 4J).

Bessie: The Third Doctor's car—a yellow roadster.

Bi-Al Foundation: Hospital space station located near TITAN in the year 5000. It was invaded by the NUCLEUS (4T).

Big Business: Often portrayed as the villain (for example, VV, HHH, TTT, 4W, 5E).

Biroc: One of the Time-sensitive THARILS. He was the navigator of slaver RORVIK's privateer, and escaped to free his people (5S).

Black Holes: They have at various times led to an ANTI-MATTER universe (RRR), powered the TIME LORDS (4P) or helped the NIMON to cross the Universe (5L).

Block Transfer Computations: Method used by the mathematicians of LOGOPOLIS to shape or recreate reality (5V).

Blood: Some life forms encountered by the Doctor depended on it for their survival; for example, the silicon-based OGRI (5C) or the GREAT VAMPIRE and his Human servants (5P).

Bloodaxe: Medieval bandit and henchman of IRONGRON (UUU).

Blue Crystal: Found by the Third Doctor on METEBELIS 3, it helped him to deliver his friends from BOSS's mind control (TTT). It magnified the mental powers of its owner and was eventually brought back to Metebelis 3 by the Doctor where it destroyed the GREAT ONE (ZZZ).

Bok: Name given to AZAL's GARGOYLE (JJJ).

Borusa: Cardinal of the TIME LORDS. A Prydonian and an old teacher of the Doctor (4P, 4Z).

BOSS (Bimorphic Organisational Systems Supervisor): Giant computer and actual head of GLOBAL CHEMICALS (TTT).

Bragen: Rebel leader of the VULCAN colony. He tried to use the DALEKS to further his own ends (LL).

Brethren: Worshippers of DEMNOS in

RENAISSANCE Italy. They were the beachhead of Mandragora (4M).

Brock: Earth agent of the Argolins. He was impersonated by the West Lodge members of the FOAMASI (5N).

Brotadac: One of the GAZTAKS and second to General GRUGGER. He died with MEGLOS (5Q).

Broton: Leader of the ZYGONS and impersonator of the Duke of FORGILL (4F).

Buckingham (Lady Jennifer): Ambulance driver during the First World War. She was a victim of the War Games (ZZ).

Cailleach: Very real Druidic goddess, alias of alien criminal, CESSAIR of DIPLOS (5C).

Caleb: Warrior of the SEVATEEM who became leader after the death of Andor (4Q).

Callufrax: Planet destroyed by ZANAK. In reality a segment to the KEY TO TIME (5B).

Cameca: Aztec lady with whom the First Doctor flirted in order to find his way back to the TARDIS (F).

Camilla: Formerly known as Navigation Officer Lauren Macmillan of the Earth ship *Hydrax*. Drawn into E-SPACE by the GREAT VAMPIRE, she became one of the immortal vampire rulers of a local planet (along with AUKON and ZARGO). She died when the Doctor destroyed the Great Vampire (5P).

Campbell (David): Earth freedom-fighter against the DALEKS. He married SUSAN, the First Doctor's granddaughter (K).

Capitol: City of the TIME LORDS (4P, 4Z).

Captain: Ex-pirate and apparent master of ZANAK, whose Bridge he designed. In reality a pawn of its Queen, XANXIA, who controlled his Cyborg half and killed him when he tried to revolt (5B).

Caris: Tigellan woman who helped the Doctor against

MEGLOS. She wanted her people to reclaim their planet's surface (5Q).

Carrington: Ex-astronaut of MARS PROBE 6. Promoted General of the Space Security Department, he attempted to start a war between the 'radioactive Martians' he blamed for the death of his companions, and Earth (CCC).

Carstairs: Lieutenant in the British Army during the First World War. He was a victim of the War Games (ZZ).

Castellan: Title given to the head of Gallifreyan security (4P, 4Z).

Catherine de Medici: She ordered the ST BARTHOLOMEW'S DAY MASSACRE (W).

Cavemen: Encountered by the First Doctor, whose companion Ian gave them the secret of fire (A).

Caven: Notorious Space Pirate (YY).

Celestial Intervention Agency: Secret organisation of the TIME LORDS which intervenes in the Universe's affairs when deemed necessary. The Doctor has been its unwilling agent (4P).

Celestial Toymaker: Mysterious entity who looks like a happy mandarin and forces space travellers to play his games—or die. He was defeated by the First Doctor (X).

Cerebretion Mentor: Device used by the CYBERMEN in their invasion of Earth (VV).

Cessair: Real name of Vivien FAY, alien criminal from DIPLOS (5C).

Chameleons: Race who lost their identities in a nuclear war. They were discovered and defeated by the Second Doctor while in the process of taking over unsuspecting Humans (KK).

Channing: A Replica, a superior Auton used by the Nestene in its attempt to take control of Earth (AAA).

Chaplet (Dodo): One of the Doctor's companions. She came from the 20th century and returned there

(W–BB).

Charged Vacuum Emboitements (CVE): They were created by the mathematicians of LOGOPOLIS to maintain the existence of our Universe. They lead into E-SPACE. THARILS used to live in the CVE zone (5R–5V).

Chase (Harrison): Mad millionaire and plant-lover. He endangered the whole Earth when he stole and grew a Krynoid (4L).

Chedaki: Marshal of the KRAALS who was sceptical of STYGGRON's plan for the invasion of Earth (4J).

Chen (Mavic): Guardian of the Solar System—and traitor: he offered a taranium core to the DALEKS, enabling them to power their TIME DESTRUCTOR, but they eventually killed him (V).

Chesterton (Ian): One of the Doctor's companions. Teacher of physics at COAL HILL SCHOOL. He and Barbara WRIGHT followed SUSAN home and met the Doctor (A–R).

China: Visited by the First Doctor in the 13th century (D) (see also FFF, KKK, 4S).

Chinn: Politician without a conscience who wanted to gain power through the use of Axonite (GGG).

Chloris: Planet with vast supplies of chlorophyll but no metal. It was ruled mercilessly by the Lady ADRASTA (5G).

Cho-Je: Tibetan monk. An avatar of Time Lord K'ANPO (ZZZ).

Chorley: Member of the press who followed the Army's operations when the YETI invaded London (QQ).

Chronic Hysteresis: Another kind of time loop. It was used by MEGLOS against the Doctor (5Q).

Chumblies: Little robots which served the RILLS and helped the Doctor to escape the fury of the DRAHVINS (T).

City: Living city built by the Exxilons. It found them imperfect and expelled them. One of the 700 Wonders

of the Universe, it was destroyed by the DALEKS
(XXX).

Clancey (Milo): Innocent yet eccentric space miner
mistaken for the infamous pirate CAVEN (YY).

Clantons: Famous Tombstone family, defeated at the
OK CORRAL (Z).

Clent: Leader of the Ice Base in the year 3000 (OO).

Clones: The Fourth Doctor and LEELA were cloned
and miniaturised in (4T). The Sontarans are a clone
race.

Coal Hill School: Attended by Susan, the First
Doctor's granddaughter, who was followed home by
two teachers who became the Doctor's companions (A).

Coligny (Admiral de): Encountered before the ST
BARTHOLOMEW'S DAY MASSACRE (W).

Colonies (in Space): (see G, R, V, Y, EE, JJ, YY,
HHH, NNN, QQQ, ZZZ, 4C, 4B, 4Q, 4T, 4W, 5A,
5E).

Company: It made the artificial suns around PLUTO.
It oppressed and exploited Mankind through unjust
taxes. It was in reality a tool of economic conquest of
the USURIANS (4W).

Condo: Servant of SOLON. He revolted after he found
that his hand had been used in the making of the
MORBIUS Monster. Solon killed him (4K).

Conscience: Giant computer controlling the island of
MARINUS absolutely equitably. It was destroyed by
YARTEK when he inserted the wrong key.

Continuous Event Transmuter: The CET Machine
could record samples of flora and fauna on laser
crystals. The samples go on living in the recording.
Naturalist TRYST used one to smuggle VRAXOIN out
of EDEN (5K).

Controller (of Earth): Servant of the DALEKS. He
rebelled and was killed by them (KKK).

Cordo: Inhabitant of PLUTO. Driven to suicide by the
burden of taxation, he was saved by the Doctor and

LEELA. He took part in the rebellion against the COMPANY (4W).

Cory (Marc): Space Special Security Service agent. He was killed on KEMBEL by the DALEKS (T/A).

Crayford (Gary): First Earth spaceman to Jupiter. He was kidnapped by the KRAALS who turned him against his own people. When he found that he had been duped, he redeemed himself and died fighting STYGGRON (4J).

Crinoth: Planet devastated by the Nimon, who were planning to leave it for SKONNOS, but because of the Doctor's intervention they were destroyed with it (5L).

Crusades: The First Doctor was there (P).

Cully: Rebellious son of the Dulcian leader. He helped the Doctor to defeat the DOMINATORS (TT).

Cutler (General): In charge of the South Pole base which was attacked by the CYBERMEN (DD).

Cybermats: Little metallic creatures used by the CYBERMEN as advanced means of attack (MM, SS, 4D).

Cybermen: Once human, they gradually replaced the organic parts of their bodies with plastics and metals. They have no emotions and are ruthlessly logical. They have the strength of ten men. Originally from MONDAS, the twin planet of Earth, they moved to TELOS, which was destroyed by the Doctor after their first invasion attempt. They then attacked the WHEEL IN SPACE and invaded the MOON Base. They tried to invade Earth with the help of INTERNATIONAL ELECTROMATICS. Later, they fought against Mankind in the galactic Cyberwars. They were almost exterminated because of one of their major weaknesses: GOLD, which is deadly to them and was found in abundance on VOGA. The Cybermen resurfaced again near space station NERVA in a final attempt to destroy Voga (DD, HH, MM, SS, VV, 4D).

Cyrennic Alliance: A federation of planets, of which

RIBOS is a member (5A).

D84: Robot detective disguised as a Dum on the SANDMINER (4R).

Daemons: Powerful race from planet Daemos. The Daemons look like the Devil in Earth mythology. They came to Earth in prehistoric times to experiment with Human civilisation. They had god-like powers. The Giant Vampires destroyed by the TIME LORDS might have been an offshoot of the Daemon race. The last of the Daemons, AZAL, was discovered on Earth by the MASTER (JJJ).

Dalekanium: Substance created and used by the DALEKS. It is, among other things, a powerful explosive (KKK).

Daleks: Created by DAVROS, the Daleks are the mutated descendants of the KALEDS, one of the two races living on SKARO (see also THALS). Genetically crippled by centuries of warfare, the Daleks live inside travel machines. They have only one purpose: to exterminate all other life forms. Their history is confusing: they attempted—sometimes with success—to invade Earth at various periods in its history. They used other races—OGRONS, DRACONIANS, etc.—and collaborated with the MASTER, Galaxy 5, etc. to further their own plans of conquest of the Galaxy. Their war with the Thals still rages on, and so does their war with the MOVELLANS, another robotic race. They developed time travel facilities. The Second Doctor created Good Daleks by contaminating them with the Human factor. A civil war followed, which almost destroyed the Dalek race. The Emperor Dalek is a super-Dalek, unable to leave Skaro. Dalek armies are usually led by a Black Dalek or a Dalek Supreme. The Doctor believes that a greater good will come out of the Daleks' creation (B, K, Q, R, T/A, V, EE, LL, KKK, QQQ, SSS, XXX,

[33]

4E, 5J).

Dallios: King of ATLANTIS. After his Queen, GALLEIA, betrayed him and allied herself with the MASTER, he died (OOO).

Dask: Alias Taren Capel. He considered robots to be his brothers, and tried to engineer a robot revolt against the Humans on the SANDMINER. He was killed by a robot which did not identify his voice (4R).

Davros: Great but twisted and crippled KALED scientist. He betrayed and caused the destruction of his race to create the DALEKS. He was killed by them but apparently survived inside a force field, for he was resurrected by his creations to help them fight the MOVELLANS (4E, 5J).

Deciders: Name given to the leaders of the starliner community on planet ALZARIUS (5R).

Deedrix: Leader of the Tigellan scientists (5Q).

Della: Assistant to space naturalist TRYST (5K).

Delta Magna: Planet whose original inhabitants were shipped to a moon (Delta 3) to make room for human colonists. Because of its growing population, a methane refinery was later installed on the Moon. Its controller, THAWN, tried to exterminate the descendants of the Deltans, now called SWAMPIES, but was killed by their god, KROLL (5E).

Demat Gun: It was used by the Doctor to save GALLIFREY from a Sontaran invasion. The Gun was activated by the GREAT KEY and channelled all the power of the TIME LORDS in a seering disintegration blast (4Z).

Demnos: Pagan god worshipped by the BRETHREN in RENAISSANCE Italy (4M).

Dent (Captain): He worked for IMC on the planet EXARIUS. A villain (HHH).

Deons: Tigellan worshippers of the DODECA-HEDRON (5Q).

Desperus: Planet where convicted murderers from

Earth were sent (V).

Devil's End: Place where Azal was discovered by the MASTER (JJJ).

De Vries: Druid and servant of the CAILLEACH. He was killed by the OGRI (5C).

Dido: Planet peopled by friendly natives. The First Doctor found VICKI there and fought KOQUILION (L).

Dinosaurs: Pets of the Silurians (BBB). Also appeared in London as a result of a misguided attempt to reverse Time (OPERATION GOLDEN AGE) (WWW).

Diplos: Planet of origin of CESSAIR, who stole the great seal of DIPLOS, in reality a segment of the KEY TO TIME (5C).

DN6: Dangerous insecticide manufactured by the evil FORESTER which could have destroyed the whole world (J).

Doc Holliday: Famous gunslinger, whom the Doctor encountered at the OK CORRAL in Tombstone (Z).

Dodecahedron: Mysterious crystal-like artefact which powered the Tigellan civilisation. It might have been created by the Zolfa-Thurans. It was stolen by MEGLOS and destroyed by the Doctor (5Q).

Dominators: Evil race of aliens who wanted to destroy the peaceful planet DULKIS to obtain radioactive waste to power their space fleet. They were instead destroyed by the Second Doctor. Their robots were the deadly QUARKS (TT).

Doomsday Weapon: Built by an ancient race that reverted to savagery, it was located on Earth colony. The Master stole a record of its location from the TIME LORDS' files. The Doctor tracked him there and managed to persuade its Guardian to destroy the weapon rather than give it to the Master (HHH).

Dortmun: Scientist who fought the DALEKS when they invaded Earth—and was killed by them (K).

Doubles of the Doctor: The DALEKS built an

Android double of the First Doctor (R), who later might have met his real-life double in the person of the ABBOT OF AMBOISE (W). The Second Doctor met his in would-be world dictator SALAMANDER (PP). The Fourth Doctor was duplicated as an Android by the Kraals (4J), gave his personality to a computer, XOANON (4Q), was cloned to fight the NUCLEUS (4T), was duplicated by the Argolins' TACHYON RECREATION GENERATOR (5N) and impersonated by MEGLOS of ZOLFA-THURA (5Q).

Draconians: The Draconians are a race of dragon-like humanoids who control a space empire rivalling Earth's in the 26th century. The MASTER and the DALEKS nearly manipulated them into a war with Mankind, which was averted when the Draconian Emperor turned out to be a friend of the Doctor (QQQ).

Dracula: Vampire. The Doctor and the DALEKS met him (or his Android counterpart) in a haunted house (R).

Drahvins: Evil aliens looking like beautiful females. They wanted to steal the RILLS' ship to flee the destruction of the planet where they crashlanded (T).

Drashigs: Ugly and vicious swamp monsters. They escaped from the SCOPE, in which they were prisoners, and created some disturbance on planet INTER MINOR (PPP).

Drax: Renegade Time Lord, builder of the MENTALIS machine of ZEOS and ally of the Doctor against the SHADOW (5F).

Duggan: Strong, abrasive British detective encountered by the Doctor in Paris. He helped him to overcome SCAROTH (5H).

Dulkis: Planet of the Dulcians, a peace-loving and advanced race threatened with nuclear extermination by the DOMINATORS. They were saved by the Second Doctor (TT).

Dwarf Star Alloy: Super heavy alloy used by slaver RORVIK to imprison the Time-sensitive THARILS (5S).

Dynatrope: Machine used by the KROTONS to turn mind power and intelligence into energy (WW).

Earp (Wyatt): Famous gunslinger encountered by the First Doctor at the OK CORRAL (Z).

Earth History:

Prehistory

c. 400 Million BC: SCAROTH's spaceship explodes, creating life on Earth (5H).

c. 200 million BC: SILURIANS and SEA DEVILS share Earth with DINOSAURS. Some Dinosaurs are drawn forward in time to the 20th century by OPERATION GOLDEN AGE. The Silurians are eventually driven underground by the appearance of the Moon (BBB, LLL, WWW).

c. 100 million BC: ELDRAD's hand arrives on Earth and becomes a fossil (4N).

c. 50 million BC: Two Krynoid pods land in the ANTARCTIC and bury themselves in the permafrost (4L).

c. 12 million BC: The FENDAHL comes to Earth. Its skull will influence Mankind's evolution (4X).

c. 1 million BC: Ice Age. A Martian exploration ship is frozen, and will remain so till AD 3000 (OO).

c. 500,000 BC: The Doctor gives the secret of fire to a tribe of CAVEMEN (A).

c. 100,000 BC: The DAEMONS find Earth. Primitive CAVEMEN paintings indicate their awesome presence (JJJ).

c. 50,000 BC: A Zygon spaceship lands in Loch Ness. The ZYGONS will remain hidden till the 1980s (4F).

c. 10,000 BC: Fall of ATLANTIS (OOO).

Antiquity

c. 5,000 BC: The OSIRIANS defeat and imprison SUTEKH in EGYPT (4G).

c. 2,500 BC: The Doctor and the DALEKS fight near the Great Pyramid (V).

c.2,000 BC: CESSAIR of DIPLOS lands on Earth and impersonates a Druidic goddess, the CAILLEACH (5C).
c.1,200 BC: The Doctor takes part in the TROJAN WAR (U).
AD 64: The Doctor is the inspiration of NERO's burning of ROME (M).
c. AD 100: A Roman legion is kidnapped by the WAR LORDS (ZZ).

Modern History
c.800: LINX, a Sontaran warrior, crashes down in England (UUU).
1066: The Doctor meets the Meddling MONK near Hastings and ensures the defeat of King HAROLD (S).
1190: The Doctor helps King RICHARD's Crusade (P).
c.1200: The Doctor visits the AZTECS (F).
c.1300: The Doctor meets MARCO POLO in CHINA and almost loses the TARDIS in a backgammon game with Kublai Khan (D).
c.1400: The Doctor spends some time in TIBET, where he meets lama PADMASAMBHAVA.
c.1500: The Dukedom of SAN MARTINO is invaded by the MANDRAGORA HELIX, then saved by the Doctor (4M). Meanwhile, because of SCAROTH's financial needs, Leonardo da Vinci is forced to paint more than one MONA LISA (5H).
1572: ST BARTHOLOMEW'S DAY MASSACRE (W).
c.1650: The Doctor meets smugglers in Cornwall (CC).
1746: The Doctor at Culloden (FF).
1792: The Doctor is involved in the FRENCH REVOLUTION (H).
c.1862: A US Civil War army is kidnapped by the WAR LORDS (ZZ).
1866: The DALEKS capture Professor WATERFIELD in London in an attempt to draw the Doctor from the 20th century (LL).
1872: The Doctor and the DALEKS are responsible for

the disappearance of the crew of the MARIE-
CELESTE (R).
1881: The Doctor at the OK CORRAL (Z).
1889: In London the Doctor confronts and defeats a
criminal from the 49th century posing as a Chinese god
(4S).
1909: On the island of FANG ROCK, the Doctor repels
a Rutan invasion (4V).
1911: The Doctor defeats SUTEKH (4G).
*c.*1915: The WAR LORDS kidnap a First World War
battlefield (ZZ).
1926: A ship to India is captured by VORG's SCOPE
(PPP).
1935: In TIBET the Doctor meets the YETI and fights
the GREAT INTELLIGENCE, which has taken over
his old friend PADMASAMBHAVA (NN).

Contemporary Adventures
1963: SUSAN goes to COAL HILL SCHOOL (A).
1964: A miniaturised Doctor stops FORESTER from
manufacturing DN6 (J).
1965: Very brief visit to the EMPIRE STATE
BUILDING (R); Ian CHESTERTON and Barbara
WRIGHT return to London (R); the Doctor spends
Christmas in Liverpool (V).
1966: The Doctor defeats WOTAN (BB) and the
CHAMELEONS (KK).
1970–75: The Doctor prevents Professor ZAROFF
from blowing up the Earth (GG). He saves a refinery
from weed creatures (RR).
1975–80: Second YETI invasion and first meeting with
LETHBRIDGE-STEWART (QQ). First CYBER-
MEN attacks (VV, DD).
1980–90: All UNIT stories (AAA–4F) and subsequent
20th-century stories (4J, 4L, 4N, 4X, 5C, etc.)

Future

1980–90: First MARS Probe (CCC). First manned rocket to Jupiter (4J).

1990–2000: Space stations. The CYBERMEN attack the WHEEL IN SPACE (SS). Development of T-MAT and weather control. First MOON Base.

c. 2000: The ICE WARRIORS invade the MOON Base (XX). Beginning of the colonisation of the Solar System. T-MAT is phased out and rockets make a comeback.

c. 2030: The Doctor foils would-be world dictator SALAMANDER (PP).

c. 2050: First contacts with other star systems. First interstellar expeditions (5R, 5P). Lost ships (ZZZ, 4Q, 5R, 5P).

c. 2070: Gravity control. The new Moonbase is attacked by the CYBERMEN (HH).

c. 2100: An alternative future in which the Daleks have conquered Earth after years of nuclear wars is erased by the Doctor (KKK).

c. 2164: Dalek invasion of Earth (K). After the DALEKS' defeat, the colonies help Earth to rebuild.

c. 2200: First colonisation attempts outside the Solar System: METEBELIS 3 (ZZZ), XOANON'S world (4Q), MECHANUS (R) etc. On Earth the depletion of natural resources, already drained to a considerable extent by the DALEKS, forces Mankind to accept the economic domination of the COMPANY, the USURIANS' tool of conquest. Mankind is forced to move to MARS, and then to PLUTO.

c. 2300: Fall of the COMPANY and return of the Human race to Earth (4Y). Outside the Solar System Mankind's colonies expand (5N).

c. 2400: Galactic Cyberwars. Mankind utilises VOGA's enormous GOLD resources to destroy the CYBER-MEN Empire. Beginning of Earth Empire.

c. 2450: An expedition to TELOS finds the Tombs of

the **CYBERMEN (MM). The Earth's Empire grows** and develops.

*c.*2500: Earth's empire is almost at war with the DRACONIANS (QQQ). A new Dalek Invasion of the Galaxy is averted (SSS).

*c.*2600: Earth's period of colonial expansion leads to conflicts with other races: the MACRA (JJ), the WIRRN (4C), the SENSORITES (G) etc. It is also the age of the SPACE PIRATES (YY).

c. 2800: The DALEKS try to blackmail Mankind with a space plague. An Earth expedition finds an antidote on EXXILON (XXX).

c. 2900: Space Station NERVA is built. Last of the CYBERMEN die near VOGA (4D). Outside the Solar System multi-planetary corporations develop their influence (HHH, 5K).

c. 3000: Ionisation fails. Earth is threatened by a new Ice Age, which is averted by the Doctor despite Ice Warrior Intervention (OO).

*c.*3100: Earth's empire starts to crumble. Planets want their independence. The SOLOS crisis is the catalyst of the change (NNN).

c. 3200: Beginnings of the FEDERATION.

*c.*3500: PELADON joins the FEDERATION (MMM).

*c.*3550: GALAXY 5 attacks the FEDERATION and attempts to gain control of PELADON's TRISILI-CATE mines (YYY).

c. 3700: The Federation grows in influence and so does Earth (PPP, 5A).

*c.*4000: The DALEKS join forces with GALAXY 5 and other galaxies to attack Earth, the now-dominant member of the FEDERATION. Their Master Plan fails when KEMBEL is destroyed by the TIME DESTRUCTOR (T/A, V).

c. 4200: Earth is evacuated to escape solar flares. Space station NERVA is turned into an ARK, which is invaded by the WIRRN (4C).

c. 4300: The Doctor defeats the WIRRN (4C) and the SONTARANS' experiment on Earth (4B). Earth is reclaimed by the Nerva people and the colonies.

*c.*4500: DALEKS fight with the MOVELLANS. DAVROS is taken prisoner to Earth (5J).

*c.*5000: TITAN base attacked by the NUCLEUS (4T). New Ice Age on Earth. Time of the Icelandic Alliance and of the ZIGMA EXPERIMENT (4S).

? The Sun goes nova. A space ARK is launched (Y).

c. 30,000: Mankind has forgotten about Earth and has formed new civilisations: MORESTRA (4H), the robot-based society on the SANDMINER (4R) etc. Even from the DALEKS, a greater good has come: benevolent Daleks created by the Doctor have replaced the evil creations of DAVROS (who might have been the last Emperor Dalek?) (LL).

Eckersley: Earth engineer working in the TRISILICATE mines on PELADON. He betrayed the FEDERATION to GALAXY 5 for money. He was killed by AGGEDOR (YYY).

Eden: Home planet of the Mandrels. A section of it was captured by TRYST in his CET Machine (5K).

Eelek: Ambitious Deputy Council Leader of the GONDS (WW).

Egypt: (see V, 4G).

Elders: Advanced race of an alien planet who lived by stealing the life energy of the SAVAGES. The Doctor made them change their ways. They elected Steven TAYLOR as their leader (AA).

Eldrad: Kastrian criminal. He destroyed the force fields he had created to protect KASTRIA against the cold ravages of space because he could not rule the planet. Destroyed by King ROKON, his hand fell on Earth and stayed there, fossilised, for centuries. It was found by Sarah Jane SMITH, and forced her to take it into a nuclear reactor where it regenerated. The Doctor took him back to Kastria, where he now reigns alone (all the Kastrians are dead). Eldrad's life form is silicon-based (4N).

Eldred (Professor Daniel): Aging rocket-builder and last of his kind on a T-MAT controlled Earth. He helped the Doctor against the ICE WARRIORS (XX).

Eleanor (Lady): Noblewoman whose castle was threatened by IRONGRON (UUU).

Elixir of Life: Produced by the Sacred Flame of KARN. It is kept by the SISTERHOOD and shared with the TIME LORDS (4K).

Emperor Dalek: Super-Dalek and Supreme Leader. He might have been a last incarnation of the evil DAVROS (LL).

Empire State Building: Briefly visited by the Doctor and the DALEKS (R).

Engin (Coordinator): Time Lord in charge of the APC Net (4P)

England: Outside the 20th century, see S, CC, LL, UUU, 4G.

Erato: Ambassador from TYTHONUS to CHLORIS, sent to arrange an exchange between his planet, rich in metal, and Chloris, rich in chlorophyll, but was captured by Lady ADRASTA and kept in a PIT. He was freed by the Doctor (5G).

E-Space: Exo-Space. Smaller universe located beyond the Charged Vacuum Emboitement. ALZARIUS the GREAT VAMPIRE's planet and the THARILS, are located in E-Space (5R–5S).

Exarius: Planet where Human Colonists opposed IMC (HHH).

Exxilon: Planet of the CITY, computerised entity which expelled its creators into wilderness. Their descendants hate technology and worship the City from outside. Some of them, a minority, appear more advanced and intelligent. The Doctor and the DALEKS fought on Exxilon for the possession of

PARRINIUM, the antidote to a galactic plague (XXX).
Eye of Horus: Device set up by HORUS on MARS to imprison his brother SUTEKH on Earth (4G).

FANG ROCK: Island where the Doctor and LEELA defeated an advanced Rutan invasion. The island itself is said to be haunted by sea creatures (4V).
Faraday: UNIT Colonel, in command when the KRAALS attempted to invade Earth (4J).
Farrel: Owner of a plastics factory and victim of the MASTER and the NESTENE (EEE).
Farrow: Government inspector murdered by Forester before he could reveal the dangers of DN6 (J).
Fay (Vivien): Alien criminal. Alias of CESSAIR of DIPLOS, she impersonated the CAILLEACH, a Druidic goddess. Vivien Fay controlled the OGRI and through the possession of a segment of the KEY TO TIME could change shape. She was turned into stone by the MEGARA (5C).
Federation: Alliance of planets which followed the collapse of Earth's empire. ARCTURUS, ALPHA CENTAURI, the ICE WARRIORS and PELADON were members (MMM, YYY).
Federico (Count): Villain. Tried to steal SAN MARTINO from its rightful ruler, GIULIANO. He was killed by Mandragora (4M).
Fendahl: Creature composed of a Core and many Fendahleens. The Fendahl feeds on life itself. It originated on the Fifth Planet of a Solar System, which was time-looped by the TIME LORDS. One of the Fendahl escaped. He may have stopped on MARS before reaching Earth in 12 million BC. He materialised with the aid of a Human medium—having influenced Human evolution to this end—but the Doctor, helped by the Tylers, destroyed his support (a skull) by dropping it near a supernova (4X).
Fendelman (Professor): Pawn of the FENDAHL. He

[44]

invented the sonic TIME SCANNER which contributed to the Fendahl's materialisation (4X).

Ffinch (Lieutenant Algernon): English lieutenant fighting the Scots at Culloden (FF).

Fibuli: Assistant to the CAPTAIN of ZANAK (5B).

Fifth Planet: Home of the FENDAHL, which was time-looped by the TIME LORDS in an attempt to destroy the Fendahl (4X).

Filer (Bill): American intelligence agent in charge of the MASTER file. He helped the Third Doctor defeat AXOS (GGG).

Fishmen: Possibly the last descendants of ATLANTIS, they were freed from Professor ZAROFF's enslavement by the Second Doctor (GG).

Foamasi: Reptilian race which fought a nuclear war with ARGOLIS. The West Lodge of the Foamasi tried to sabotage the Argolins' LEISURE HIVE but were unmasked by Foamasi government agents, who made peace with Argolis (5N).

Forester: Mad scientist and industrialist. His DN6 insecticide almost destroyed all life on Earth. He was stopped by a gas explosion engineered by an ant-size Doctor (J).

Forgill (Duke of): Scottish nobleman impersonated by BROTON. He was the President of the Scottish Energy Commission (4F).

France: (see H, W, 5H).

Frankenstein's Monster: The First Doctor and the Daleks met him, or his Android counterpart in a haunted house (R).

French Revolution: The First Doctor was there (H).

Galaxy 5: It had a part in the Daleks' Master Plan (V). It also fought a war against the FEDERATION and tried to sabotage the mining of TRISILICATE on PELADON (YYY).

Galaxy 4: Location of the planet of the RILLS and the

DRAHVINS (T).

Galleia: Queen of ATLANTIS and wife of DALIOS. Seduced by the Master, she betrayed her King. She later turned against the renegade Time Lord and perished in the destruction of ATLANTIS (OOO).

Gallifrey: Home planet of the TIME LORDS, it is located in the Constellation of Kasterborus. Its coordinates from galactic zero centre are: 10–0–11–00 by 02. The name of Gallifrey was introduced in (UUU) but the planet was glimpsed previously in (ZZ, HHH, RRR) and became the theatre of operations in (4P) and (4Z). Gallifrey appears to be divided in highly sophisticated cities, such as the CAPITOL, where Time Lords live, and vast areas of wilderness, peopled by tribes of SHOBOGANS. Gallifrey is powered by the energies of a supernova (RRR), and/or of a captive black hole (4P). It was almost destroyed by OMEGA (RRR) and by the MASTER (4P). It was later invaded by the VARDANS and the SONTARANS (4Z), but the Doctor managed to save it in each instance.

Galloway (Dan): Ruthless Scottish weapons officer and member of the expedition trying to find an antidote to a space plague on EXXILON. He betrayed the expedition but redeemed himself by sacrificing himself to destroy a Dalek ship (XXX).

Gargoyle: Creature animated by AZAL the Daemon. Also called BOK (JJJ).

Garif: One of the DECIDERS of ALZARIUS (5R).

Garron: Earth con-man. He and his friend UNSTOFFE tried to sell RIBOS to the GRAFF VYNDA-K (5A).

Gatherer Hade: Tax collector for the COMPANY on PLUTO. He was killed by the crowd during the uprising (4W).

Gaztaks: Gang of space raiders led by General GRUGGER. They followed MEGLOS to his doom (5Q).

Gebek: Leader of the miners on PELADON. At the

suggestion of the Third Doctor, he became Chancellor (YYY).

Giuliano: Rightful ruler of the Dukedom of SAN MARTINO in RENAISSANCE Italy (4M).

Global Chemicals: Multinational corporation managed by BOSS. It was responsible for the GREEN DEATH (TTT).

Gold: Found in abundance on VOGA. It was deadly to CYBERMEN (4D).

Gonds: Peaceful aliens. The most intelligent Gonds were used by the Kroton Machine to bring its masters back to life. After the Second Doctor destroyed the KROTONS the Gonds went back to their happy life (WW).

Goth (Chancellor): Time Lord, Prydonian—and traitor! He killed the President, because he had been passed over for succession and because he had listened to the MASTER's promises of power. He was murdered by the Master after his defeat at the Doctor's hands inside the APC Net (4P).

Grant (Jo): One of the Doctor's companions. She joined UNIT as Assistant to the Third Doctor and left him to marry Professor Clifford JONES (EEE to TTT).

Gravitron: Gravity-controlling machine installed on the MOON Base. It could control Earth's weather—or defeat the CYBERMEN (HH).

Great Intelligence: Cosmic entity which attempted twice to conquer Earth. Its favourite pawns appeared to be the robot YETI which were animated by silver spheres contained in their chests. The Great Intelligence could take over the minds of any Earthman. It was almost siphoned by the Doctor's mind when it tried to drain the Time Lord's brain (NN, QQ).

Great Key: Created by RASSILON, it was a symbol of the presidency of Gallifrey, along with the Rod of Rassilon, the Sash of Rassilon and the MATRIX. The

Great Key had been entrusted to the Cardinal. For the first time in recorded Time Lord history it was in the possession of a President when Borusa handed it to the Doctor. The Great Key activates the DE-MAT GUN (4Z). Another version of it (or was it the Rod?) opened the chambers leading to the black hole kept captive under the PANOPTICON (4P). That version was stolen by the Master.

Great One: Giant Spider of METEBELIS 3. She was destroyed by the energies released when she achieved completion of her crystal web with the BLUE CRYSTAL (ZZZ).

Great Vampire: See Vampires (5P).

Greel (Magnus): War criminal from the year 5000. He fled back in time through the unsuccessful ZIGMA EXPERIMENT, which crippled him and forced him to steal the life energies of others to survive. He arrived in CHINA and posed as a local god, WENG-CHIANG. He and his servitor LI HSEN CHANG moved to London, where he was killed in 1889. His body disintegrated as a result of cellular collapse (4S).

Green Death: Giant maggots and green slime created by the toxic industrial waste released by GLOBAL CHEMICALS and pumped into an abandoned mine (TTT).

Grendel (Count): He attempted to steal Prince REYNART's throne on the planet TARA (5D).

Grey: Crooked solicitor who tried to sell captive Scots as slaves (FF).

Grover (Sir Charles, MP): Mastermind behind OPERATION GOLDEN AGE. He was the victim of his own plan (WWW).

Grugger (General): Leader of the GAZTAKS. He perished with MEGLOS in the explosion of the DODECAHEDRON (5Q).

Guardian: Last descendant of the race who created the DOOMSDAY WEAPON. He destroyed it, and himself, at the Doctor's suggestion (HHH).

Guardians of Time: There are at least two of them: the White Guardian on the side of Order and the Black Guardian on the side of Chaos, but their exact nature, role and powers are yet unclear. The White Guardian enlisted the help of the Doctor and Romana to reconstitute the KEY TO TIME and restore the universal balance. The Black Guardian confronted the Doctor after the Time Lord had reassembled the Key. Thwarted by the Doctor, he swore to have his revenge on the Time Lord. To escape the Black Guardian, the Doctor equipped the TARDIS with a RANDOMISER (5A, 5F).

Gundans: Axe-wielding robots built by the THARILS' slaves to withstand the time winds and free them from their masters. After the Tharils' capture, the Gundans were left to guard the gates into E-SPACE (5S).

Habris: Chief of the guards of King ZARGO and Queen CAMILLA of the E-SPACE planet of the GREAT VAMPIRE. He was killed by IVO (5P).

Hamilton (Lieutenant Peter): Member of the expedition trying to locate an antidote to a space plague on EXXILON. He survived to bring the antidote back to Earth (XXX).

Hardin: Earth scientist who, with the help of ROMANA, perfected the Argolins' TACHYON RECREATION GENERATOR and rejuvenated MENA (5N).

Harold (King): He almost won at Hastings because of the Meddling MONK's interventions (S).

Hawthorne (Miss): Local white witch who alerted the Third Doctor to the evil at DEVIL'S END (JJJ).

Hensell: Governor of the VULCAN colony (EE).

Hepesh: High Priest of PELADON. He was very much against Peladon joining the FEDERATION and used AGGEDOR—and ARCTURUS—in an attempt to prevent it from doing so (MMM).

Herrick: Member of the Minyan party searching for the P7E (4Y).

Hieronymous: Court Astrologer of SAN MARTINO. He was a Priest of DEMNOS and led the BRETHREN after he became possessed by the MANDRAGORA HELIX (4M).

Hildred: Bungling commander of the CAPITOL Guards from GALLIFREY (4P).

Historical Adventures of the Doctor: (D, F, H, M, P, R, U, V, W, Z, CC, FF, UUU, 4G, 4M, 5H).

Hobson: Head of the Moon base (HH).

Horda: Vicious animals used in a test of heresy by the SEVATEEM (4Q).

Horus: Leader of the OSIRIANS. He imprisoned his brother SUTEKH on Earth (4G).

Huntsman: Master of the carnivorous Wolf Weeds of CHLORIS, he served and eventually revolted against the Lady ADRASTA (5G).

Hymetusite: Radioactive crystals and source of energy. They were part of the tribute paid by ANETH to the NIMON on SKONNOS (5L).

Hyperspace: Dimension used for fast space travel (for example, 5B, 5C, 5K).

Ice Warriors: Martians. They are huge green scaly creatures, equipped with sonic guns and armour. They are extremely sensitive to heat—their only weakness. Their leaders appear to be slightly sleeker and less bulky. A group of them, under the leadership of VARGA, visited Earth in its prehistoric past and were frozen during the Ice Age. They were found in the year 3000 by the Second Doctor (OO). The Ice Warriors, under the leadership of SLAAR, also attempted to invade Earth with Martian Seed Pods (XX). Later they became part of the Galactic FEDERATION and their

Ambassador to PELADON, IZLYR, helped the Third Doctor against ARCTURUS (MMM). A renegade Ice Warrior, AZAXYR, betrayed the Federation to GALAXY 5 on the same Peladon (YYY). It is likely that the Ice Warriors left MARS to start a new, more peaceful life on another planet in the Galaxy.

Interplanetary Mining Corporation (IMC): It attempted to seize control of the planet EXARIUS from its rightful colonists by using underhanded tactics (HHH).

Inferno: Project aiming at penetrating the Earth's crust and releasing a new source of energy (STAHLMAN's Gas). It was masterminded by Professor Stahlman and almost caused the destruction of Earth (DDD).

Insects: Insect-like aliens were encountered by the Doctor on several occasions (N, TTT, ZZZ, 4C).

Inter Minor: Extremely xenophobic world, recently opened to other planets (PPP).

International Electromatics: Multinational corporation controlling most of the world's computers and managed by Tobias VAUGHN. It helped the CYBERMEN in an invasion attempt (VV).

International Space Corps: Earth space patrol particularly active against pirates (YY).

Invasions of Earth: (see K, V, DD, KK, LL, NN, QQ, VV, XX, AAA, EEE, GGG, 4C, 4F, 4J, 4M, 4V).

Ion Bonder: Weapon used by the Doctor.

Ioniser: The Doctor used one to defeat the Ice Warriors and postpone the second ice age (OO).

Irongron: Medieval war lord and bandit. He allied himself with LINX (UUU).

Isotope: Following the Doctor's instructions Barbara WRIGHT used one to destroy the ANIMUS (N).

Issigri (Dom): Dom Issigri was the ex-partner and prisoner of the SPACE PIRATE CAVEN. His daughter, Madeleine, first allied herself with Caven and then reformed (YY).

Ivo: Leader of the peasants of the vampire planet (5P).

Ixta: Chosen warrior of the Aztecs (F).

Izlyr: Ice Warrior Ambassador to PELADON. He helped the Third Doctor to unmask the treachery of ARCTURUS (MMM).

Jabel: Leader of the TESH and servant of XOANON (4Q).

Jackson (Ben): One of the Doctor's companions. A true cockney sailor (BB–KK).

Jackson: Or, as the Doctor called him, Jason! Leader of the Minyan expedition engaged in a 100,000-year quest for the P7E (4Y).

Jagaroth: War-like race of green aliens with one red eye which perished when SCAROTH's spaceship exploded on Earth (5H).

Jago (Henry Gordon): Owner of a London theatre in the 19th century, under which WENG-CHIANG had his lair. He helped the Doctor and Professor LITE-FOOT to defeat the Chinese god (4S).

Jamie (McCrimmon): One of the Doctor's companions. Young piper of clan laird Colin McLAREN, he joined the Time Lord after the defeat of the Scots in 1746. He was transported back to his own era by the TIME LORDS (FF–ZZ).

Janis Thorn: Poisonous plant causing paralysis and death in its victim. Favourite weapon of LEELA (4Q).

Jano: Leader of the ELDERS. He adopted some of the Doctor's attitudes after he stole his life energy (AA).

Jethrik: One of the most precious minerals in the Galaxy. A lump of it owned by GARRON was the first segment of the KEY TO TIME (5A).

Jones (Professor Clifford): Nobel prize ecologist. He helped the Third Doctor to defeat BOSS and the GREEN DEATH. He married Jo GRANT and they went on an expedition on the Amazon river (TTT).

Jovanka (Tegan): One of the Doctor's companions.

This young Australian air hostess accidentally entered the TARDIS after her aunt's murder at the hands of the MASTER. She found herself in LOGOPOLIS and stayed with the Doctor (5V).

K9: A dog-like mobile computer equipped with advanced weapons, tracking systems, etc. It was built by Professor MARIUS in the 49th century and followed the Doctor and LEELA after their battle with the Nucleus (4T). The original K9 stayed on GALLIFREY with Leela after the Sontaran Invasion (4Z). A new improved K9 Mark 2 was then assembled by the Doctor. It proved to be very helpful in the quest for the KEY TO TIME but later suffered many mishaps (including a spell of space laryngitis). It was partially destroyed by the time winds and had to remain in E-SPACE with ROMANA to keep functioning (4T–5F, 5G–5S).

Kaftan: One of the members of the archaeological expedition looking for the Tombs of the CYBERMEN on TELOS. She was instrumental in their release (MM).

Kal: Caveman (A).

Kaleds: Ancestors of the DALEKS—and enemies of the THALS. They were destroyed by a Thal rocket following the betrayal of DAVROS, creator of the Daleks (4E).

Kalik: INTER MINOR commissioner who plotted the overthrow of his superior by the use of the SCOPE (PPP).

Kalmar: Rebel scientist on the GREAT VAMPIRE's planet (5P).

K'Anpo: Ancient Time Lord and mentor of the Doctor on GALLIFREY. He lived on Earth as a Tibetan monk. He reincarnated as his servant, CHO-JE, during the METEBELIS 3 affair. He helped the Doctor to regenerate and reach his fourth incarnation (ZZZ).

Karn: Planet of the SISTERHOOD, keepers of the Sacred Flame. In centuries past, the renegade Time Lord MORBIUS attacked it with an army of outcasts, but he was defeated and subsequently disintegrated. Later the Doctor fought a resurrected Morbius and rekindled the Sacred Flame. Karn is in the same galaxy as Gallifrey (4K).

Kassia: Wife of TREMAS of TRAKEN. She was manipulated by the MASTER and turned against her husband. The Master killed her to become KEEPER OF TRAKEN (5T).

Kastria: Home planet of ELDRAD. Kastrians are silicon-based life forms who evolved from sentient rocks to humanoid shape. Their planet was barren and ravaged by space winds. To protect it Eldrad built force fields, which he later destroyed. For this crime King ROKON sentenced him to death. Kastria is now totally deserted, except for Eldrad (4N).

Katarina: One of the Doctor's companions. She joined the TARDIS crew during the TROJAN WAR and sacrificed herself to prevent the Doctor from being blackmailed in his fight against the DALEKS (U–V).

Keara: One of the OUTLERS on ALZARIUS (5R).

Keeper of Traken: Guardian of the Bioelectronic Source of the Union of TRAKEN, from which it derives immense powers. The MASTER succeeded in becoming Keeper—but was defeated by the Doctor (5T).

Keller (Professor): Alias of the MASTER when he built the machine which was inhabited by a MIND PARASITE (FFF).

Kellman: Greedy scientist working on space station NERVA. He appeared to be working for the CYBERMEN but was really working for the Vogans (4D).

Kelner: CASTELLAN of GALLIFREY, he betrayed the TIME LORDS once to the VARDANS and once to the SONTARANS (4Z).

Kembel: Planet from which the DALEKS prepared to launch their Master Plan. It was ravaged by the TIME DESTRUCTOR (T/A, V).

Kent (Giles): He tried to kill the Second Doctor in his attempts to seize power from would-be world dictator SALAMANDER (PP).

Kerensky (Professor): Scientist whose time travel experiments were financed by SCAROTH, who killed him (5H).

Kettlewell (Professor): Builder of the Giant Robot and secret member of THINK TANK. He was killed by his creation (4A).

Keys of Marinus: Five artefacts enabling their bearer to control the CONSCIENCE. Ian found a fake key, which destroyed the Conscience, thwarting the VOORDS (E).

Key to Time: All-powerful artefact which enabled the bearer to control Time itself. Shaped like a cube, the Key is divided into six segments, scattered throughout the Cosmos. The White Guardian sent the Doctor in search of them to avert Chaos and restore the balance of the Universe. The segments were disguised as a lump of JETHRIK, the planet Callufrax, the great seal of DIPLOS, a holy relic of the SWAMPIES, a Taran statue and Princess ASTRA of ATRIOS. After his dramatic confrontation with the Black Guardian the Doctor scattered the segments again (5A–5F).

Khrisong: Tibetan warrior (NN).

Kingdom (Sara): Sister of Bret VYON, who was killed because of the DALEKS' machinations, she joined the Doctor and died in the TIME DESTRUCTOR armaggedon on KEMBEL (V).

Klieg: Responsible for the CYBERMEN's resurrection on TELOS (MM).

Koquilion: Apparently a benevolent creature from the planet DIDO; in reality Bennett, murderer of an Earth spaceship crew and 'friend' of VICKI (his alibi) (L).

Kraals: Alien race who attempted to invade Earth with the help of ANDROIDS built by their chief scientist STYGGRON (4J).

Krang: Cyberleader who led the attack on the South Pole base in the 1980s (DD).

Krasis: Priest of Poseidon and Guardian of the KRONOS Crystal in ATLANTIS (OOO).

Kroll: Originally a small, squid-like creature brought by the Human colonists to Delta Magna's third moon. Swallowing the fifth segment of the KEY TO TIME made it grow to gigantic size. It was adored as a god by the SWAMPIES. After its attack on the methane refinery, it was neutralised by the Doctor who removed the segment (5E).

Kronos: Mysterious entity, leader of the Kronovores, who lives in the time vortex and seems to feed on Time itself. The MASTER attempted to control its powers but in vain. Released, Kronos destroyed ATLANTIS but saved the Doctor who had freed it. At the Doctor's request it spared the Master (OOO).

Krotons: Crystalline life forms whose system is based on telurium. They fed on the GONDS' intelligence until they could live again. Brought back to life by the Doctor's brain power, the Krotons tried to capture and harness the Time Lord. The Doctor used acid to destroy them (WW).

Krynoids: Intelligent form of plant life. The Krynoids travel in pairs through Space as pods. When they arrive on a planet, they are able to absorb animal life forms and grow to gigantic size before germinating. They can control other planets. Two pods were discovered, buried in the ANTARCTIC permafrost. One of the Krynoids was destroyed by the Doctor. The other one, stolen by CHASE, was bombed by the RAF after it had reached a monumental size, just before germination (4L).

Kublai Khan: The Doctor played backgammon with him and won 35 elephants, 4,000 horses, 25 tigers—but lost the TARDIS key (D).

Ky: Solonian. He became first a Mutant and then turned into a super-Solonian, the next stage in their evolution (NNN).

Land of Fiction: Realm where characters from fantasy live. It was controlled by a giant computer and a man called the MASTER, who wanted to take over Earth so that it could provide them with endless new fictions. The computer was destroyed by ZOE (UU).

Latep: Member of the Thal expedition to SPIRIDON (SSS).

Lazlo: One of the Time-sensitive THARILS. He was instrumental in the release of his race (5S).

Leela: Savage warrior from the SEVATEEM tribe. She became one of the Doctor's companions, and stayed on GALLIFREY after marrying ANDRED (4Q–4Z).

Leeson: Colonist who was killed fighting against IMC (HHH).

Leisure Hive: Artificial environment created by the Argolins to entertain visitors and promote inter-racial understanding. The Hive almost went bankrupt because of the machinations of the West Lodge members of the FOAMASI, who were planning to buy it. It was saved by the Doctor and some agents of the Foamasi Government, who invested in the Hive (5N).

Lesterson: Chief scientist from the VULCAN colony. He thought he could control the DALEKS (EE).

Lethbridge-Stewart (Brigadier Alistair): He conceived the idea of UNIT while he was a Colonel in the British forces fighting with the Doctor against the YETI. Later he became the head of the British branch of UNIT and shared many adventures with the Third Doctor. He never quite understood the Doctor or his TARDIS. The Doctor's faculty to regenerate upset him enormously (QQ, UU, AAA, BBB, CCC, DDD, EEE, FFF, GGG, HHH, JJJ, KKK, OOO, RRR, TTT, UUU, WWW, ZZZ, 4A, 4F).

Lexa: Leader of the DEONS on TIGELLA. She sacrificed herself to save ROMANA (5Q).

Li Hsen Chang: Chinese magician and hypnotist who was given super-normal powers by his master, WENG-CHIANG, whom he rescued in China. Because of his inability to kill the Doctor, Weng-Chiang turned against him. He eventually became the victim of his former master's pet: a giant rat (4S).

Linx: Sontaran warrior who landed in the middle ages and gave modern technology to warrior IRONGRON (in the form of a robot knight) so that he could help him to repair his spaceship. He captured 20th century scientists and drew the attention of the Doctor. He was eventually defeated by the Time Lord and his local allies, and killed by an arrow (UUU).

Litefoot (Professor): English scientist who owned Weng-Chiang's time cabinet. He helped the Doctor and Mr JAGO defeat the Chinese 'god' (4S).

Llanfairfach: Location of the GLOBAL CHEMICALS plant that released the toxic waste which turned some maggots into the GREEN DEATH (TTT).

Loch Ness Monster: In reality a Skarasen, semi animal-cum-robot built by the ZYGONS and used in their attempt to take over Earth (4F).

Login: One of the DECIDERS of ALZARIUS (5R).

Logopolis: City of Logic inhabited by pure mathematicians whose block transfer computations could recreate any object or preserve the Universe beyond the point of normal heat death. Logopolis was destroyed by the MASTER, but its program, run on the Pharos Computer on Earth, kept the Universe alive (5V).

Lowe: Head of the Titan base. He was taken over by the NUCLEUS (4T).

Lupton: Member of a Tibetan Meditation Centre, he

allied himself with the SPIDERS of METEBELIS 3 in the quest for the BLUE CRYSTAL. He was eventually killed by the Spiders (ZZZ).

McLaren (Colin): Clan laird of JAMIE (FF).
Macra: Giant crab-like beings who secretly controlled an Earth colony, making it appear to be very happy. They lived on gas produced by the colonists and died when the Second Doctor cut their supplies (JJ).
Magrik: Vogan Leader. Unlike General VORUS, he favoured a policy of secrecy to protect the Vogans from the CYBERMEN (4D).
Mailer (Harry): Convict at STANGMOOR Prison. He was used by the MASTER in an attempt to start the Third World War (FFF).
Maitland (Captain): Captain of the Earth spaceship kept prisoner by the SENSORITES (G).
Mandragora Helix: Mysterious energy life form which lies in the time vortex. It seems to feed on magic, superstition and the adoration of its servants. Unaware of its presence, the Doctor took it to RENAISSANCE Italy, where it took over the BRETHREN (who worshipped the pagan god DEMNOS) and tried to kill all the great minds of the time. Its energy was drained by the Doctor but it will be in position to attack Earth again in the late 20th century (4M).
Mandrel: (1) Leader of the underground fighters on PLUTO (4W). (2) Mud monsters from the planet EDEN captured by TRYST and unleashed on the ship *Empress* after a malfunction of the CET Machine. When they are destroyed, their essence is revealed to be VRAXOIN (5F).
Marco Polo: The Doctor met him in CHINA (D).
Maren: Leader of the SISTERHOOD. She sacrificed herself to save the Doctor's life (4K).
Marinus: Planet where the First Doctor and his companions land on an island of glass sand in a sea of acid.

Controlled equitably by the CONSCIENCE. It was later invaded by the alien VOORDS (E).

Marius (Professor): Professor from New Heidelberg, the Bi-Al Foundation in the year 5000. He built the original K9 and helped the Fourth Doctor defeat the NUCLEUS (4T).

Mars: Fourth Planet of the Solar System. Home of the ICE WARRIORS in prehistoric times (OO) and possibly in our near future (XX). References to the Ice Warriors mention them as Martians but they could have emigrated to another planet in the Galaxy. The FENDAHL attacked Mars while en route to Earth (4X). HORUS of the OSIRIANS built a pyramid on Mars to hide the EYE OF HORUS, a device which kept his brother SUTEKH prisoner on Earth (4G). Lastly, the Humans moved to Mars and established a temporary colony—secretly controlled by the USURIANS—after having depleted Earth's natural resources. They later moved to PLUTO (4W).

Marshal: (1) Sadistic leader of the Earth colony of SOLOS. He was killed by KY (NNN). (2) Responsible for ATRIOS's defence against ZEOS. He was time-looped by the Doctor (5F).

Marie-Celeste: The Doctor landed there briefly. The DALEKS followed—which explains the mysterious disappearance of the crew (R).

Master (of the Land of Fiction): Mysterious elderly man who served the giant computer that was actually in charge of the Land. He wanted the Doctor to replace him (UU).

Master: Renegade Time Lord and sworn enemy of the Doctor, he is a deadly hypnotist. His trademark is to murder people with a gun which compresses their atoms, leaving doll-sized corpses. He allied himself at various times with the NESTENE, AXOS, the DALEKS, and other aliens, to try to conquer or to destroy Earth (the Master likes destruction for its own sake). He was always defeated by the Doctor but inevitably managed to escape. He was imprisoned only once, on Earth, following the AZAL affair but broke jail with the help of the SEA DEVILS (LLL). The Master eventually used up his twelve regenerations and almost caused the death of GALLIFREY in a mad attempt to steal the energy necessary to start a new life cycle. Although the Doctor saved the planet of the Time Lords, the Master escaped. He eventually achieved his ends by merging with the body of TREMAS of TRAKEN after having become the Keeper of the Union. He was defeated again. Later he almost caused the end of the Universe by destroying LOGOPOLIS. He and the Doctor joined forces to run the Logopolis program on the Pharos Computer on Earth. The Master tried to blackmail the Universe but the Doctor managed to save the day, at the cost of his fourth body (EEE, FFF, GGG, HHH, JJJ, LLL, OOO, QQQ, 4P, 5T, 5V).

Matrix: One of the symbols of the presidency on GALLIFREY. It is a crown enabling its wearer to achieve a direct link with the APC Net (4P, 4Z).

Maxtible (Theodore): Victorian scientist, who helped the DALEKS to isolate a Human factor. He was later infected by the Dalek factor and became evil. He was killed by one of the Doctor's friends when the Time Lord and his companions fled SKARO (LL).

Mechanoids: Robots sent to colonise the planet Mechanus. They became its masters instead. The Mechanoids started a space zoo in which they kept space travellers—including Steven TAYLOR. They were destroyed by the DALEKS (R).

Medok: One of the Colony members who fought the MACRA (JJ).

Megara: Slightly single-minded justice machines built by an alien race. They judged their creators in contempt of court and destroyed them. They were prisoners on

CESSAIR's ship in hyperspace and were inadvertently released by the Doctor when he broke into their cells. They placed him on trial for this crime. They were later banished by the Doctor after they had tried Cessair and turned her into stone (5C).

Meglos: Last of the Zolfa-Thurans, Meglos's natural form resembles a cactus. He used the GAZTAKS and impersonated the Doctor to steal TIGELLA's DODECAHEDRON. He died in an explosion arranged by the Doctor (5Q).

Melkur: Name given by the Trakens to the evil calcified beings on their planet. The MASTER himself was a Melkur until he managed to free himself and become Keeper (5T).

Mena: Leader of ARGOLIS and 'mother' of Pangol. She was rejuvenated by HARDIN's Tachyon machine (5N).

Menoptera: Butterfly-like aliens from the planet VORTIS. They fought alongside the First Doctor to regain their planet invaded by the ANIMUS and the ZARBI (N).

Mentalis: Giant computer of ZEOS. It was built by DRAX (5F).

Mentiads: Telepathic life form who originated on ZANAK. They helped the Doctor to stop the pirate planet (5B).

Merak: Chief Surgeon of ATRIOS. He helped the Doctor to save Princess ASTRA from the SHADOW (5F).

Metal Virus: Used by the Doctor to destroy Professor KETTLEWELL's Giant Robot (4A).

Metebelis 3: Blue planet of the Acteon Galaxy. The Doctor found it to be very hostile and full of vicious blue animals (TTT). A crystal picked up there proved to be the missing piece searched by the GREAT ONE, a giant Spider who controlled the descendants of the Human colonists on the planet. The SPIDERS were destroyed by the Doctor (ZZZ).

Mind Parasite: Entity feeding on evil thoughts and inhabiting the KELLER Machine built by the MASTER. It was destroyed by the Third Doctor (FFF).

Minerals: They played an important part in many stories. As natural resources, especially if rare, they can become the object of passions—like the MOLYBDENUM of SENSE-SPHERE (G), the PARRINIUM of EXXILON (XXX), the TRISILICATE of PELADON (YYY), the ANTI-MATTER of ZETA MINOR (4H) or the GOLD from VOGA (4D). One should also mention minerals or metals with peculiar properties such as the multi-purpose DALEKANIUM (KKK) or the super-heavy DWARF STAR ALLOY which kept the Time-sensitive THARILS prisoner (5S). Some minerals confer great powers on their owners, such as the TARANIUM Core which powered the Daleks' TIME DESTRUCTOR (V), the KRONOS Crystal from ATLANTIS (OOO), the BLUE CRYSTAL from METEBELIS 3 (TTT, ZZZ), GARRON's lump of JETHRIK (5A), the HYMETUSITE crystals so important to the NIMON (5L) or the Tigellan DODECAHEDRON (5Q). The most important piece of crystal of all was the KEY TO TIME (5A–5F). Some life forms are mineral-based such as the telurium-based KROTONS (WW), the silicon-based Kastrians (4N) or the blood-absorbing OGRI (5C). Some planets depend heavily on minerals for their existence: ZANAK (5B) and CHLORIS (5G) are two examples. The planet TYTHONUS was very rich in minerals (5G).

Miniaturisation: (see J, KK, PPP, 4T, 5F).

Minotaur: Encountered by the Second Doctor (UU). Guardian of the KRONOS Crystal in ATLANTIS, it was defeated by the Third Doctor (OOO). The Nimon resemble minotaurs (5L).

[63]

Minyos: The TIME LORDS helped the Minyans to develop their civilisation but the Minyans destroyed each other in nuclear wars. A second planet, Minyos 2, was colonised by the survivors as a second chance for the Minyan race. Jackson and his crew spent 100,000 years searching for the Minyan Race Banks carried by the long-lost vessel P7E. The Doctor helped them to find the Race Banks and return to Minyos 2 with other Minyans who had been kept enslaved by the ORACLE (4Y).

Mira: Planet located near KEMBEL and inhabited by the VISIANS, giant, invisible, hostile aliens (V).

Molybdenum: SENSE-SPHERE was rich in it and consequently feared Human exploitation (G).

Mona Lisa: Painted many times over by Leonardo da Vinci to help SCAROTH's plans (5H).

Mondas: Twin planet of Earth, it was the CYBER-MEN's home planet. When they attempted to invade Earth in the late 1980s, it was destroyed by the First Doctor (DD).

Monitor: Head of LOGOPOLIS, he was the victim of the MASTER's schemes (5V).

Monk (Meddling): Renegade Time Lord first encountered by the Doctor in 1066. He wanted to 'improve' Human history by giving atomic bazookas to King HAROLD. After some adventures in Ancient Egypt with the DALEKS, he was tricked by the Doctor who stole his TARDIS directional unit and left him stranded on an ice planet (S, V).

Monoids: They started as slaves to the Humans of the Space Ark but became their masters because of a cold introduced by DODO (Y).

Moon: Earth's Moon was the location of a base, which first controlled the T-MAT system (XX) and was later invaded by the Cybermen (HH). It may have become a penitentiary later on (QQQ).

Morbius: Time Lord of the first rank, he betrayed

GALLIFREY by leading an army of outcasts to attack the planet KARN, promising them life eternal if they could steal the SISTERHOOD's Elixir. He was defeated and his body was publicly disintegrated—but his brain survived! Later, Solon transplanted it into a monstrous body after having failed to obtain the Doctor's. The brain of Morbius was destroyed in a mental duel with the Doctor and the body was destroyed by the Sisters (4K).

Morestra: Planet of humanoids whose expedition on ZETA MINOR was attacked by an ANTI-MATTER creature (4H).

Moroks: War-like race who conquered many other races and set up a space museum on XEROS (Q).

Movellans: They look like beautiful, peaceful humanoids but they are in reality a robot race whose hostility rivals the DALEKS'—with whom they are at war (5J).

Mummies: The First Doctor wrapped up the Meddling MONK in mummy cloths. (V). SUTEKH's mummies were in reality Osirian Service ROBOTS (4G).

Mutters Spiral: Another name for the Milky Way Galaxy.

Napoleon Bonaparte: Encountered by Ian and Barbara during the FRENCH REVOLUTION (H).

Neeva: Priest of XOANON (4Q).

Nefred: One of the DECIDERS of ALZARIUS. He knew the truth about his people and died when the marshmen attacked the starliner (5R).

Neman: Proctor of TRAKEN. He served KASSIA and after her death the MASTER (5T).

Nero: The Doctor inspired him to burn Rome (M).

Nerva: Original name of the space station first used as a beacon in orbit around VOGA and then turned into a space Ark (4C, 4B, 4D).

Nesbin: Former Time Lord and leader of the SHOBOGANS. He helped the Doctor and LEELA fight the SONTARANS (4Z).

Nestene Consciousness: Cosmic intelligence whose true shape looks like a cross between a crab and an octopus. It has a special affinity with plastics and uses Autons and Replicas to conquer planets. In its second attempt to take over Earth it allied itself with the MASTER (AAA, EEE).

Nimon: Alien species which resembles the MINOTAUR. Like a galactic plague of locusts, they travelled through Space leaving behind wasted planets and conquering new ones by sending an advance emissary who promises untold riches to unsuspecting worlds. The Doctor defeated them on SKONNOS (5L).

Noah: Leader of the crew of the space Ark, he was taken over by the WIRRN but fought back and sacrificed himself to destroy the invaders (4C).

Nova Device: Machine used by the MOVELLANS to destroy the atmosphere. They attempted to blow up SKARO with one (5J).

N-Space: Normal Space. Our Universe. It was endangered by OMEGA (RRR). Later it was revealed that it had passed the point of normal heat death and was maintained by the block transfer computations of the mathematicians of LOGOPOLIS (5V).

Nyder: Assistant to DAVROS. He was killed by the DALEKS (4E).

Nyssa: One of the Doctor's companions. Daughter of TREMAS of TRAKEN, Nyssa was taken to LOGOPOLIS after her father's death by the mysterious WATCHER. She remained with the Doctor (5T, 5V).

Nucleus: Of the VIRUS of the Purpose. Microscopic space entity who took over the Doctor and a host of people from the TITAN base. Having been thrown out of the Time Lord's body and having assumed Human proportions, it tried to swarm on Titan but was destroyed when the Doctor blew up the base (4T).

Ogri: Silicon-based life forms from the TAU CETI System, they feed on blood. Three of them came to Earth with Vivien FAY and served her while posing as a part of a Druidic stone circle. They were destroyed by the MEGARA (5C).

Ogrons: Very strong ape-like beings with a limited intelligence who originated on a bleak, desolate planet. They were the henchmen of the DALEKS (KKK, QQQ).

Ohica: One of the SISTERHOOD, she believed in the Doctor (4K).

OK Corral: (see Z).

Omega: One of GALLIFREY's first time engineers. He blew up the star which became known as the Crab Nebulae to give the TIME LORDS the energy necessary to start time travel (this appears to be in contradiction with the RASSILON myths, which state that the energy of the Time Lords comes from a captive black hole). Omega was believed dead after the ensuing cosmic explosion and was made a hero of Gallifrey. In reality he had escaped and lived on, prisoner of an ANTI-MATTER universe where he was able to create a whole world by the very power of his mind. Wanting to leave his prison, Omega used a black hole to drain the Time Lords' energy and bring a Time Lord—in this instance, the Doctor—to him. But he was too late: his physical form had disappeared, destroyed by the anti-matter, and only his mind remained. To prevent his annihilating the Universe out of sheer despair, the Three Doctors, brought together by the Time Lords, put Omega into contact with the Second Doctor's recorder, the only artefact composed of positive matter in Omega's universe. The resulting supernova replenished the Time Lords' energy sources (RRR).

Operation Golden Age: Plan to turn back the clock of Time and plunge Earth back into the prehistoric times. The plan was masterminded by Sir Charles Grover and Professor Whitaker (WWW).

Oracle: Super-computer in charge of the Minyan vessel P7E. It went crazy and created its own world at the edge of the Universe composed of its slaves, the TROGS, and its guards, the SEERS. It fought the Doctor and the Minyans when they tried to take back the Minyan Race Banks it was supposed to protect. It was destroyed in an explosion of its own making, intended to kill Jackson (4Y).

Organon: Court Astrologer of the Lady ADRASTA of CHLORIS (5G).

Ortron: Chancellor of Queen THALIRA on PELADON. He was killed by the ICE WARRIORS (YYY).

Orum: INTER MINOR commissioner who, together with KALIK, plotted the overthrow of his superior by the use of the SCOPE (PPP).

Osirians: God-like race from PHAESTER OSIRIS who are now extinct. They created Egypt's mythology when HORUS and the rest of the Osirians fought and defeated SUTEKH (4G).

Outlers: Name given by the starliners to the people who refused to follow the DECIDERS. ADRIC and his brother VARSH were Outlers (5R).

P7E: Spaceship which fled Minyos just before its extinction, carrying with it the Race Banks which were the promise of a better future on Minyos 2. The ship was lost because of its computer, the ORACLE. After a 100,000-year quest Jackson and the Doctor found it and recovered the Race Banks, despite interference from the Oracle (4Y).

Packard: Second Officer of RORVIK's privateer ship (5S).

Padmasambhava: Tibetan lama and old friend of the Doctor. He was taken over by the GREAT INTELLIGENCE (NN).

Pangol: Believed to be the Argolin 'son' of MENA, he was in fact a creation of the TACHYON RECREATION GENERATOR. After having taken over ARGOLIS, Pangol attempted to duplicate himself into an army, but was stopped by the Doctor. He was later rejuvenated by accident to an infant stage (5N).

Panopticon: The great hall of ceremonies of the TIME LORDS. Located in the CAPITOL. Directly beneath it lies Rassilon's captive black hole (4P, 4Z).

Paris: Trojan warrior (U).

Parrinium: Cure to a Dalek space plague found on EXXILON (XXX).

Parry (Professor): Head of the expedition which discovered the Tombs of the CYBERMEN on TELOS (MM).

Peking Homunculus: See Mr SIN (4S).

Peladon: (1) Planet rich in TRISILICATE. It joined the FEDERATION despite a plot hatched by High Priest HEPESH. One generation later it was threatened by another plot involving dissident ICE WARRIORS in cahoots with Galaxy 5. (2) King of the planet. His mother was an Earth-woman. His daughter, THALIRA, succeeded him. (MMM, YYY).

Phaester Osiris: Home planet of the OSIRIANS (4G).

Pharos Project: Earth computer and radio-telescope project whose aim was to beam messages and contact other life forms. It was copied by the LOGOPOLIS mathematicians in their attempts to preserve the existence of the Universe. After Logopolis's death, the Doctor and the MASTER used the Pharos Computer to run the Logopolis program (5V).

Ping-Cho: Chinese girl (D).

Pluto: Location of an Earth colony ruled secretly by the USURIANS. It was warmed by artificial suns. It was

abandoned after the revolt against the Usurians'
COMPANY (4W).

Polly: One of the Doctor's companions. Professor
Brett's secretary, she and Ben Jackson joined the
Doctor in his adventures—and returned exactly one day
later (BB–KK).

Polyphase Avatron: Mechanical bird used by the
CAPTAIN of ZANAK as a weapon (5B).

Pralix: One of the MENTIADS of ZANAK (5B).

Prapilius: Old MENOPTERA scientist (N).

Prehistory: see EARTH HISTORY.

Primords: Ape-like creatures created by STAHL-
MAN's GAS (DDD).

Probes 6 and 7: Earth spaceships sent to MARS. *Probe
6* met radioactive aliens and of its crew only Carrington
survived. The *Probe 7* crew disappeared and another
ship, *Recovery 7*, was sent after it. It was later found
that the aliens were not hostile (CCC).

Prydonians: One—some say the best—of the TIME
LORDS' Colleges. Its colour is scarlet. The Doctor,
BORUSA and GOTH were all Prydonians. They are
said to be devious (4P).

Quarks: Deadly robots serving the DOMINATORS
(TT).

Radnor (Commander): T-MAT Supremo. He was
instrumental in re-establishing the use of rockets after
the ICE WARRIORS' T-MAT invasion (XX).

Rago: One of the DOMINATORS' leaders (TT).

Randomiser: Device attached by the Doctor to the
TARDIS to confuse the Black Guardian about his
movements. It was later accidentally destroyed by the
Doctor after he used it to randomise Pangol's duplicates
(5N).

Ranquin: Leader of the SWAMPIES. He was killed by
KROLL (5E).

Ransome (Thea): Scientist assisting Professor
FENDELMAN. She was a medium and became the
FENDAHL Core (4X).

Rassilon: First of the TIME LORDS. The legends
around his life and deeds date back to the very origins of
GALLIFREY. He went into a black hole, captured it
and imprisoned it under the PANOPTICON. This is
supposedly the major source of power of the Time
Lords. Rassilon also built the oldest and strongest force
fields around Gallifrey (which were later supplemented
by the TRANSDUCTION BARRIER). He created the
symbols of power worn by the President: the MATRIX
(link to the APC Net), the Sash (a device enabling its
wearer to protect himself from the black hole energies),
the Rod and the GREAT KEY (which can be used to
gain access to and harness the energies of the hole). This
aspect of the Rassilon story appears to contradict the
OMEGA legends. Rassilon is also credited with having
destroyed the Great Vampires (using bowships). He
ordained that the story be preserved in the Records of
Rassilon, which used to be kept in all old TARDISes
(4P, 4Z, 5P).

Rebec: Member of the Thal expedition to SPIRIDON
(SSS).

Recovery 7: Spaceship sent to MARS to discover what
had happened to *Probe* 7. Its crew was replaced by
radioactive aliens (CCC).

Reegan: Ex-convict who was used by General
CARRINGTON in his plans to start a war between
Earth and the radioactive aliens (CCC).

Refusis: Final destination of the space ARK. The
Refusians helped the Humans to make peace with the
MONOIDS (Y).

Renaissance: (4M, 5H).

Renegade Time Lords: Name generally given to the
TIME LORDS who left GALLIFREY to pursue
ambitions of their own. Among those are the Doctor, of

course, but also the Meddling MONK (S, V), the WAR CHIEF of the War Lords (ZZ), the MASTER and DRAX (5F). To this list we must add K'ANPO/ CHO-JE, who appeared to have chosen Earth as a place for retirement (ZZZ) and the SHOBOGANS, led by NESBIN (4Z). Evil Time Lords who betrayed their own race include OMEGA (RRR), MORBIUS (4K), Chancellor GOTH (4P) and Castellan KELNER (4Z).

Replica: Sophisticated Auton which can pass for a Human. CHANNING was one (AAA).

Reuben: Guardian of the FANG ROCK lighthouse. He was killed by a Rutan who took his form (4V).

Reynart (Prince): Prince of TARA, he was the victim of a plot by Count GRENDEL to steal his throne by the use of ANDROIDS (5D).

Ribos: Planet of the CYRRENIC ALLIANCE. Its ellipsis is unequal so that it enters a winterphase periodically, during which it is covered by ice. Its level of technology is roughly the equivalent of Earth's in the middle ages (5A).

Richard (the Lionheart): Encountered by the First Doctor during the Crusades (P).

Rills: Non-Human aliens who were threatened by the DRAHVINS. The First Doctor found that they were the ones who were trustworthy and good and helped them and their robots, the CHUMBLIES, to escape the destruction of their planet (T).

Ringo (Johnny): Famous gunslinger encountered by the Doctor at the OK CORRAL (Z).

Robomen: Men turned into walking zombies by the DALEKS (K).

Robots: Intelligent sentient robots like the MECHANOIDS (R), the MOVELLANS (5J) or Professor KETTLEWELL's Giant Robot (4A) seem to be the exceptions. Most robots or Androids encountered by the Doctor and his companions appear to be no more than mere programmed machines (although they sometimes display amazing proof of initiative); for example the Ice Soldiers of MARINUS (E), the DRACULA and FRANKENSTEIN'S MONSTER ANDROIDS or the Doctor's android double built by the Daleks (R), the CHUMBLIES (T), WOTAN's mobile extension, the War Machines (BB), the CYBERMATS, the GREAT INTELLIGENCE's YETI (NN, QQ), the QUARKS (TT), the LAND OF FICTION's White Robots or Clockwork Soldiers (UU), IMC's robot (HHH), LINX's Robot Knight (UUU), his fellow Sontaran STYRE's robot (4B), SUTEKH's mummies (4G) or the WHEEL IN SPACE's SERVO-ROBOT (SS). Other ANDROIDS which could duplicate life include those made by the KRAALS (4J) or the Tarans (5D). The so-called Robots of Death on the SANDMINER were divided into three categories: Dums, Vocs and Super-Vocs. Only the last two could talk and only the Super-Vocs appeared to think on their own (4R). The CAPTAIN of ZANAK (5B) and the ORACLE's SEERS (4Y) are Cyborgs, a mixture of Man and machine, as the ZYGONS' SKARASEN was a combination of animal and machine (4F). One should not forget robot pets such as K9 or the POLYPHASE AVATRON (5B). Last but not least, the axe-wielding GUNDANS were built by the THARILS' slaves to be impervious to the time winds and destroy their masters (5S). See also SUPER-COMPUTERS.

Robson: North Sea gas refinery boss who did not believe the Second Doctor's warnings about the threat of the Weed (RR).

Rodan: Young Time Lord who escaped with LEELA into Gallifreyan's wilderness, fleeing from the Sontaran invasion. At the Doctor's instruction and with the help of K9, she assembled the De-Mat Gun (4Z).

Rohm-Dutt: Gun smuggler on DELTA MAGNA's moon. He was secretly employed by THAWN and was killed by KROLL (5E).

Rokon: King of KASTRIA, he sentenced ELDRAD and joined his race in death (4N).

Romana: Lady Romanadvoratrelundar of GALLIFREY is one of the Doctor's companions. She joined him after the White Guardian, assuming the appearance of the President of the Time Lords, sent her after the KEY TO TIME. Tortured by the SHADOW, her body regenerated and she assumed the appearance of Princess ASTRA of ATRIOS. She eventually left the Doctor to help the newly freed THARILS to fight slavery in E-SPACE (5A–5S).

Rome: Burned by NERO—because of an accident caused by the First Doctor's glasses (M).

Rorvik: Space slaver. He kept all the Time-sensitive THARILS prisoner in a DWARF STAR ALLOY ship. The Tharils were freed by BIROC and LAZLO. Rorvik died in the explosion of his ship when he tried to blast his way out of a CVE (5S).

Rubeish (Professor): 20th century absent-minded scientist captured by LINX (UUU).

Rumford (Professor Amelia): Unwary friend of Vivien FAY. She helped the Doctor to defeat the villainess and her servants, the OGRI (5C).

Rutans: Blob-like amphibious species which feed on electricity and can change shape. They are engaged in a galactic war with the SONTARANS (UUU). An advanced Rutan invasion of Earth was defeated by the Doctor and LEELA on the island of FANG ROCK (4V).

Sacred Flame: It produces the ELIXIR OF LIFE, and it kept by the SISTERHOOD of KARN. It almost died and was rekindled by the Doctor (4K).

Saladin: Moslem chief during the CRUSADES (P).

Salamander: Would-be world dictator who created 'natural' catastrophes to achieve his ends. He looked exactly like the Second Doctor. He tried to steal the TARDIS but was ejected into Space because of the isomorphic nature of the TARDIS's controls (PP).

Salamar: Young leader of the Morestran expedition on ZETA MINOR. He proved to be incompetent and was replaced by VISHINSKY (4H).

St Bartholomew's Day Massacre: (see W).

Sandminer: Giant mobile factory peopled by a minimal crew of Humans and operated mostly by robots. It was the theatre of operations when a mad scientist, DASK, attempted to engineer a robot revolt (4R).

San Martino: Dukedom in RENAISSANCE Italy invaded by the MANDRAGORA HELIX. Its rightful ruler is young GIULIANO (4M).

Savages: Race used by the ELDERS who stole their life energies (AA).

Scarlioni (Count and Countess): Count Scarlioni was one of SCAROTH's 12 split personalities. The Countess was killed by Scaroth when she discovered his true nature (5H).

Scarman (Professor Marcus): British Egyptologist killed by SUTEKH who used his body to destroy the EYE OF HORUS. His brother was also killed by Sutekh (4G).

Scaroth: Last of the JAGAROTH. His spaceship exploded on Earth in 400 million BC, splitting his body in 12 parts and scattering them throughout EARTH HISTORY. To make himself whole again, he influenced Earth's development and financed Professor KERENSKY's time experiments. The Doctor discovered that the explosion of Scaroth's spaceship had created life on Earth and was able to prevent Scaroth from destroying the whole of Mankind by ensuring that the explosion took place (5H).

Scorby: CHASE's henchman. He was killed by the KRYNOIDS (4L).

Scope: Miniaturised peepshow of the Galaxy life forms.

The one which captured the TARDIS on INTER MINOR contained Humans, CYBERMEN, DRASHIGS and OGRONS (PPP).

Scotland: The Doctor was there, near Culloden, in 1746 (FF) and again at Tulloch, near the Loch Ness, in the 20th century (4F).

Sea-Devils: Undersea race of SILURIANS. They were awakened and used by the MASTER. The Navy destroyed them (LLL).

Security Chief: One of the War Lords. He was suspicious of the WAR CHIEF (ZZ).

Seeds: Martian seeds emitting a lethal fungus were used by the ICE WARRIORS in their plans for the conquest of Earth (XX). They were destroyed by rain. Later, Krynoid pods were found buried in the ANTARCTIC permafrost (4L).

Seeker: Ribosian witch with the power to track down things or people (5A).

Seers: Humans grafted with robot elements serving the ORACLE (4Y).

Selris: Gond leader who was deposed by EELEK (WW).

Sense-Sphere: Planet rich in MOLYBDENUM and home of the SENSORITES (G).

Sensorites: Telepathic aliens who feared for their safety when Earth spaceships started to explore their planet. Their existence was kept a secret by Captain MAIT-LAND (G).

Senta: ELDER scientist (AA).

Servo-Robot: Maintenance robot encountered by the Second Doctor in a space station (SS).

Seth: Young Anethian sent to SKONNOS as tribute to the NIMON (5L).

Sevateem: LEELA's tribe. They were the descendants of an Earth survey team. Their god XOANON made them fight with their brothers the TESH (4Q).

Shadow: Servant of the Black Guardian. He engineered

the war between ZEOS and ATRIOS. He turned the Doctor's friends against him and tortured Romana (5F).

Sharrel (Commander): Movellan Commander in charge of the SKARO expedition (5J).

Shaw (Liz): Cambridge scientist recruited by the Brigadier. She assisted the Third Doctor during his first months at UNIT (AAA–DDD).

Shobogans: Time Lords who rejected the Time Lord society and chose instead to live in the Gallifreyan wilderness. They helped the Doctor defeat the Sontaran invasion of Gallifrey. Their leader was NESBIN (4Z).

Shrievenzales: Ferocious animal, native of RIBOS(5A).

Shura: Guerilla fighter from the 22nd century where the DALEKS successfully invaded Earth. He killed 20th century diplomat Sir Reginald Styles, thinking to avert the Third World War but instead caused it to happen. The Doctor gave him a chance to correct his mistake and set history on the right track (KKK).

SIDRATs: Sort of second-rate TARDISes given by the WAR CHIEF to the War Lords (ZZ).

Silurians: Original inhabitants of Earth. Reptile race who went underground when the MOON arrives, isolating Earth from heat and cosmic rays. One of their characteristics is a highly developed third eye through which they can focus destructive energies. A caveful of them and their pet DINOSAURS came back to life at WENLEY MOOR, but they were bombed by the Brigadier. Sea Devils were also Silurians (BBB, LLL).

Silurian (Old, Young): Two unnamed members of the Silurian race who played a vital part in the WENLEY MOOR conflict. The Old Silurian wanted peace with Mankind while the Young Silurian prepared a deadly virus to depopulate Earth and attempted to destroy the Van Allen Belt (BBB).

Sin, Mr: Name given by Weng-Chiang to his Android,

the Peking Homunculus, a robot built in the year 5000 with the cortex of a pig. It hated Mankind and reveled in insane destruction. Its plug was pulled out by the Doctor (4S).

Sisterhood: Women gifted with super-powers who guarded the SACRED FLAME from which derived the ELIXIR OF LIFE. This they shared with the TIME LORDS. The Sisters lived on the planet KARN and were twice involved in the MORBIUS affair. The High Priestess MAREN sacrificed herself to save the Doctor. OHICA is now High Priestess (4K).

Skarasen: Giant monster, half-animal, half-robot, built by the ZYGONS. It is also known as the LOCH NESS MONSTER. After having been used by its Masters in their unsuccessful attempt to conquer Earth, it returned to the Loch (4F).

Skaro: Home planet of the THALS, the KALEDS and the DALEKS. It was ravaged by centuries of nuclear warfare between Thals and Kaleds. It is not clear whether it was dominated by the Thals (B, SSS), the Daleks (LL, 5J), or both (4E).

Skonnos: Planet which in the past controlled a vast space empire. The NIMON promised to return it to its former glory. It was levying a tribute on the planet ANETH (5L).

Slaar: Leader of the ICE WARRIORS. He attacked the MOON Base and was planning to send deadly Martian SEEDS to Earth through the T-MAT system. His physical appearance was less bulky than that of his fellow Martians (XX).

Slyther: Creature which lived in the pit dug by the DALEKS in Bedfordshire (K).

Smith (John): Name used sometimes by the Third Doctor on Earth (AAA).

Smith (Sarah Jane): One of the Doctor's companions. A journalist, she came to UNIT to investigate the disappearance of scientists. The Doctor brought her back to England, possibly to South Croydon, when he was summoned back to GALLIFREY (UUU–4N).

Smythe (General): Masqueraded as a British general during the First World War in the War Games (ZZ).

Soldeed: Leader of SKONNOS and High Priest of the NIMON (5L).

Solon: Famous galactic surgeon. He and his servant CONDO built a new body for the brain of MORBIUS on KARN (4K).

Solos: Planet dominated by the Earth Empire. As it was gaining its freedom, its natives entered a new stage of evolution, caused by Solos's cyclical rotation, turning them first into Mutants and then into super-beings (NNN).

Sondergaard (Professor): Human anthropologist on SOLOS (NNN).

Sonic Screwdriver: One of the Doctor's basic tools, along with his 500-year diary, his jelly babies, etc.

Sontarans: Militaristic clone race engaged in an age-old war with the RUTANS. They feed on energy, and have the strength of many men. According to the Doctor they can breed at the incredible rate of a million per minute! Their only vulnerable point is the probic vent behind their neck. A lone Sontaran reached Earth during the middle ages (UUU). They tried to invade Earth after the solar flares but first tried to determine the Human potential for resistance (4B). They used the VARDANS in an attempt to invade GALLIFREY (4Z).

Sorenson (Professor): Scientist from MORESTRA, he was looking for new energy sources on the planet ZETA MINOR. He experimented with ANTI-MATTER and turned into a vampiric Neanderthal-like monster. He was saved by the Doctor, who convinced him to look at the movements of planets as a source of energy (4H).

Source: Bioelectronic power source of the peaceful Union of TRAKEN. It is controlled by the Keeper.

The MASTER was able to use the Source for his thirteenth regeneration (5T).

Space Pirates: They plagued the Earth's space empire. One of the most notorious was CAVEN (YY).

Spandrell: CASTELLAN of GALLIFREY, he helped the Doctor defeat the MASTER and GOTH (4P).

Spiders: The Spiders came to METEBELIS 3 along with the Human colonists. The environment made them grow to giant size. They enslaved and fed on the Humans. The Doctor overcame them and destroyed the GREAT ONE (ZZZ).

Spiridon: Planet peopled by a race that had the secret of invisibility. One of its most interesting features was an Icecano—an ice volcano. The DALEKS kept a frozen army on Spiridon; they were defeated by the Doctor and the THALS (SSS).

Stael: One of Professor FENDELMAN's assistants, he tried to help the FENDAHL's materialisation—an act which cost him his life (4X).

Stahlman (Professor): Creator of the INFERNO Project, which aimed to penetrate the Earth's crust to release a new source of energy: Stahlman's Gas. In achieving his ends Stahlman endangered the whole Earth and was turned into a PRIMORD (DDD).

Stangmoor: Prison whose convicts were used by the MASTER in an attempt to acquire the deadly THUNDERBOLT NERVE GAS MISSILE. It was also plagued by the MIND PARASITE (FFF).

Starliner: Earth spaceship which crashed into planet ALZARIUS, located in E-SPACE. Its original passengers were killed by marshmen, who later evolved to replace them and founded a Human community, led by the DECIDERS, whose aim was to preserve the ship for its eventual departure (5R).

Stevens: Manager of GLOBAL CHEMICALS, he was under the control of BOSS (FFF).

Stimson: HARDIN's assistant—and con-man. He was

killed by West Lodge members of the FOAMASI (5N).

Stirling (James): English master spy posing as French official Lemaitre during the French Revolution (H).

Stor: Head of the Sontaran expedition which invaded GALLIFREY. He was destroyed by the Doctor (4Z).

Strella: Princess of TARA who looked exactly like ROMANA (5D).

Styggron: Chief Scientist of the KRAALS, he designed the ANDROIDS and attempted to conquer Earth. He was killed by a virus of his own making (4J).

Styles (Sir Reginald): 20th-century diplomat. Guerilla-fighters from the future thought he was to blame for the wars which enabled the DALEKS to conquer Earth—whereas in fact it had been his death, caused by SHURA, which had started the wars (KKK).

Styre: Sontaran field-major who experimented with Humans on Earth after the solar flares. He was killed by the Doctor (4B).

Sullivan (Harry): Navy Doctor and one of the Doctor's companions attached to UNIT (4A–4F, 4J).

Summer (Sir Charles): British civil servant who helped the First Doctor defeat WOTAN (BB).

Super-Computers: The CONSCIENCE of MARINUS was one but was not hostile (E). WOTAN, on the other hand, built by Professor Brett, proved a dangerous enemy (BB), and so did the computer in charge of the LAND OF FICTION (UU), the Kroton Machine (WW), BOSS (TTT), XOANON, the schizophrenic computer created by the Doctor (4Q), the Minyan ORACLE (4Y) or the MENTALIS Machine, created by DRAX on ZEOS (5F).

Susan: Sometimes called Susan Foreman because of the name given by Ian to the Doctor after they first met (it was the name of the owner of the junkyard where the TARDIS first materialised). She was the first Doctor's granddaughter. She fell in love with freedom-fighter David Campbell and remained on Earth in the 21st century (A–K).

Sutekh: Brother of HORUS and last of the OSIRIANS, he almost escaped his prison because of Egyptologist Marius SCARMAN. The Doctor caught him in a time tunnel and sent him to the end of Time where he died (4G).

Swampies: Green humanoids descendants of the original inhabitants of DELTA MAGNA. They live on Delta Magna's moon and worship their god KROLL. They were in conflict with the personnel of a methane refinery (5E).

Ta: Planet where the Second Doctor hid Milo CLANCEY, unjustly accused of being a SPACE PIRATE (YY).

Tachyon Recreation Generator: Pride of the Argolin science. This machine could create living images, such as PANGOL. It was perfected by HARDIN and ROMANA, and used to rejuvenate MENA (5N).

Tancredi (Captain): One of SCAROTH's 12 split identities. He forced Leonardo da Vinci to paint many Mona Lisas (5H).

Tara: Planet where civilisation is patterned after a chivalristic society. Science is left to the peasants. Tarans have a reputation for building life-like ANDROIDS (5D).

Tarak: One of the rebel scientists on the planet of the GREAT VAMPIRE in E-SPACE (5P).

Taranium: Precious mineral given by Mavic CHEN to the DALEKS to power their TIME DESTRUCTOR (V).

TARDIS: Acronym for *T*ime *A*nd *R*elative *D*imensions *I*n *S*pace, machines used by TIME LORDS to travel in Time and Space. Their uses are usually strictly controlled but a few TARDISes have been stolen from GALLIFREY: the MONK's, the WAR CHIEF's, the MASTER's and of course the Doctor's. TARDISes are immensely larger inside than outside because of their transdimensional nature, which also causes most weapons to become non-functional inside. TARDISes are visually invulnerable to outside attack and are protected by force fields. When attacked by overwhelming forces, a TARDIS can dematerialise and rematerialise after the attacker is gone. They can, however, be moved or transported by outside forces. They are equipped with all sorts of circuits, including a chameleon circuit which enables them to blend in safely with their environment. One can enter a TARDIS only if one is in possession of its key (which can be a trionic device or an old-fashioned key). TARDISes appear to be almost semi-sentient. The Doctor's TARDIS is an old Type 40 and was undergoing repairs on Gallifrey when he 'borrowed' it. Its chameleon circuit is stuck into the shape of a London police box and its steering mechanism is faulty and behaves in an erratic fashion. To escape from the Black Guardian, the Doctor attached a RANDOMISER to the TARDIS, but it is now left behind on ARGOLIS. The TARDISes can be controlled from afar by the Time Lords. The Doctor's TARDIS—under more or less normal gravity conditions—is reported as having a weight of (10×10) power 5 kilos. SIDRATs are second-rate TARDISes built by the War Chief for the War Lords (A, C, S, V, X, LL, PP, WW, ZZ, HHH, OOO, RRR, PPP, 4G, 4M, 4N, 4Z, 5B, 5F and 5V).

Taron: Doctor in charge of the Thal expedition to SPIRIDON (SSS).

Tau Ceti: Star system from which CESSAIR and the OGRI originated (5C).

Taylor (Steven): One of the Doctor's companions. He joined the TARDIS crew on Mechanus, where he was a prisoner, and left it to become the leader of the ELDERS (R–AA).

Tegana: Tartar warrior encountered by the First

Doctor in CHINA (D).

Telepathy: The Time Lords are supposed to be mildly telepathic. Other races displaying signs of telepathy or mind powers were the SENSORITES (G), the ANIMUS (N), the CELESTIAL TOYMAKER (X), the NESTENE (AAA, EEE), the SILURIANS (BBB), the Solonian super-beings (NNN), the SPIDERS of METEBELIS 3 (ZZZ), SUTEKH the Osirian (4G), the SISTERHOOD of KARN (4K), ELDRAD of KASTRIA (4N), the TESH (4Q), Thea RANSOME, the FENDAHL Core (4X), the VARDANS (4Z) or the SEEKER of RIBOS (5A). The LAND OF FICTION was based on a form of mind-reading (UU). The GREAT INTELLIGENCE (NN, QQ) was *all* mind. The MIND PARASITE fed on evil thoughts (FFF). The BLOCK TRANSFER COMPUTATIONS of the mathematicians of LOGOPOLIS might have been an advanced form of mind powers (5V).

Telos: Planet colonised by the CYBERMEN— and location of their deadly Tombs (MM).

Temmosus: Thal leader. He was killed by the DALEKS (B).

Tesh: Human descendants of an Earth spaceship. They had developed extra-normal mental powers and were at war with their brothers the SEVATEEM because of their 'god' XOANON, in reality a computer (4Q).

Thalira (Queen): Daughter of King PELADON and queen of the planet Peladon when its TRISILICATE mines were threatened by the renegade ICE WARRIORS (YYY).

Thals: Deadly enemies of the KALEDS, they were able to destroy them with a super-rocket because of DAVROS's betrayal. They then evolved into a perfect, peace-seeking race, but had to fight for their very survival against Davros's legacy: the DALEKS. They were masters of their home planet, SKARO, when the Third Doctor met them again on SPIRIDON (B, SSS,

4E).

Tharils: Time-sensitive race who lived in the CVE zone between E-SPACE and N-SPACE. They used to roam the time winds and enslave humanoids. They were defeated and captured by the GUNDANS, giant robots made by their own slaves. Enslaved and kept prisoner in DWARF STAR ALLOY chains by RORVIK, they were freed by BIROC. They returned to live in E-Space with ROMANA and K9 (5S).

Thascales (Professor): Alias of the MASTER when he built TOM-TIT (OOO).

Thawn: Scientist in charge of the methane refinery of DELTA MAGNA's moon. He wanted to exterminate the SWAMPIES and was killed by VARLIK (5E).

Think Tank: Evil group of scientists under the leadership of Miss Winters who prepared to take over the world with the help of Professor KETTLEWELL's Giant Robot (5A).

Thunderbolt Nerve Gas Missile: Dangerous weapon which was supposed to be dumped at sea by UNIT but was hijacked by the MASTER who wanted to use it to start the Third World War (FFF).

Tibet: The Doctor met his friend PADMASAM-BHAVA there in the 15th century and again in the 1930s, when he fought the YETI (NN). K'ANPO, a retired Time Lord, adopted the life style of a Tibetan monk (ZZZ).

Tigella: Sister planet of ZOLFA-THURA, where the aggressive vegetation forced the Tigellans under-ground. It was powered by the DODECAHEDRON. After it was stolen by MEGLOS the Tigellans started to reclaim their planet's surface (5Q).

Tigus: Volcanic planet where the Doctor met the MONK while trying to escape from the DALEKS (V).

Time Destructor: Supreme weapon of the DALEKS. It was powered by a TARANIUM Core and could destroy Time itself (V). It was operated on KEMBEL.

Time Loop: Favourite weapon of the TIME LORDS (GGG, PPP, 4X, 4Z, 5F).

Time Lords: Special caste of Gallifreyans who, after proper training at the Academy, are put in charge of monitoring the happenings of Time and Space. They rarely interfere in other races' affairs since their unfortunate experience with MINYOS. The Time Lords' origins are shrouded in mystery. RASSILON is generally known as the first Time Lord (see also OMEGA). The Time Lords destroyed the FENDAHL's race and the Great Vampires, but now they leave such interference to their secret branch, the CELESTIAL INTERVENTION AGENCY—and to free agents such as the Doctor. Time Lords are divided into Colleges such as the Prydonians (the most famous one), the Arcalians, the Patrexes, etc. The Time Lords live in the CAPITOL on GALLIFREY, which was threatened by the MASTER, the VARDANS and the SONTARANS. They were shown as a static, slightly decadent, civilisation. Time Lords have two hearts, a bypass respiratory system, a body temperature of 60°F and can regenerate their bodies 12 times. (ZZ, EEE, HHH, NNN, RRR, 4E, 4K, 4P, 4X, 4Z, 5P). See also RENEGADE TIME LORDS.

Time Scanner: Professor FENDELMAN's invention, it enabled the FENDAHL to materialise (4X).

Time Scoop: Built by Professor WHITAKER, it enabled Sir Charles GROVER to prepare OPERA-TION GOLDEN AGE (WWW).

Titan: Moon of Saturn and location of a space base which was taken over by the NUCLEUS and subsequently destroyed by the Doctor (4T).

Tlotoxl: Aztec High Priest of Sacrifice (F).

T-Mat: Instant transportation system. It was first controlled from the MOON Base and used by the ICE WARRIORS for their own deadly ends (XX). A later version of T-MAT was used to provide transportation from and to space station NERVA (4C, 4B, 4E, 4D).

Toba: One of the DOMINATORS (TT).

Tomas: Friend of LEELA and warrior of the SEVATEEM (4Q).

Tom-Tit: Acronym for Transmission of Matter through Interstitial Time, device built by the MASTER to enable him to steal the KRONOS Crystal (OOO).

Tong of the Black Scorpion: Chinese secret society which was the instrument of the will of WENG-CHIANG (4S).

Toos: Member of the SANDMINER crew (4R).

Torbis (Chancellor): Chancellor of PELADON, he favoured the admission of the planet to the FEDERATION. He was killed by AGGEDOR (MMM).

Traken (Union of): Group of planets living in perpetual harmony because of the bioelectronic SOURCE controlled by the Keeper. Evil beings calcify into MELKUR on Traken. After the death of the Keeper, the MASTER (himself a Melkur) took over the Union but was defeated by the Doctor and NYSSA (5T).

Transduction Barriers: Force fields protecting GALLIFREY (4Z).

Travers (Professor and Ann): Friends of the Second Doctor. He and his daughter Ann helped the Doctor against the YETI (OO, QQ, VV).

Tremas: One of the Consuls of TRAKEN, husband of KASSIA and father of NYSSA. He should have succeeded the Keeper but for the MASTER's schemes. His body was used by the Master for his thirteenth regeneration (5T).

Trenchard: Warden of the prison where the MASTER was kept. He betrayed his trust (LLL).

Trisilicate: Important mineral abundant on MARS and PELADON (YYY).

Trogs: Descendants of the Minyan Crew of the P7E,

they were enslaved by the ORACLE. They escaped with JACKSON (4Y).

Trojan War: The First Doctor was there—and caused the fall of Troy (U).

Tryst: Space naturalist who captured a section of the planet EDEN on his CET Machine. He was revealed to be a VRAXOIN smuggler (5K).

Tyler (Dr): Earth scientist who accompanied the Three Doctors into Omega's ANTI-MATTER universe (RRR).

Tyler (Martha and Jack): Martha Tyler was a local white witch who, with the help of her son Jack, helped the Doctor to defeat the FENDAHL (4X).

Tylos: One of the Alzarian OUTLERS (5R).

Tyssan: Earth starship engineer who was captured by the DALEKS to work on SKARO. He helped the Doctor defeat DAVROS and the MOVELLANS (5J).

Tythonus: Planet rich in metals but poor in chlorophyll. Its ambassador, ERATO, tried to arrange an exchange with CHLORIS but was thwarted by its ruler, Lady ADRASTA. Tythonians look like giant blobs, feed on chlorophyll and have no larynxes (5G).

Undersea Menaces: These include the fishmen from ATLANTIS enslaved by Professor ZAROFF (GG), the deadly Weed (RR), the SEA DEVILS (LLL), the ZYGONS' SKARASEN (4F) and the RUTANS (4V).

UNIT: Acronym for United Nations Intelligence Taskforce. UNIT is a multi-national military force based in Geneva and created to fight extra-terrestrial threats. It was the idea of Lethbridge-Stewart after the YETI invasion of London. He later became the head of its British branch (VV, AAA, BBB, CCC, DDD, EEE, FFF, GGG, HHH, JJJ, KKK, OOO, RRR, TTT, UUU, WWW, ZZZ, 4A, 4F, 4G, 4J).

Unstoffe: Earth con-man and GARRON's friend (5A).

USA: Visited twice by the First Doctor (R, Z).

Usurians: Weed-like creatures controlling a space empire based on capitalism and extortion. They can change their shape. The Doctor brought down their operations on PLUTO (4W).

Uvanov (Commander): Captain of the SANDMINER (4R).

Vaber: Member of the Thal expedition to SPIRIDON. He was killed by the DALEKS (SSS).

Vampires: Great, powerful race of winged, blood-sucking creatures (perhaps an off-shoot of the Daemon race?) destroyed by RASSILON and the TIME LORDS' bowships. Their leader, the GREAT VAMPIRE, fled into E-SPACE. He later drew the Earth ship *Hydrax* there and turned its officers, ZARGO, AUKON and CAMILLA, into his immortal vampire servants. He was killed when the Doctor drew a spaceship through his heart (5P).

Varan: Solonian tribe chieftain who collaborated with the evil MARSHAL (NNN).

Vardans: Creatures capable of travelling along any wavelength including thought. They were the pawns of the SONTARANS in their invasion of GALLIFREY. Their home world was time-looped by the Doctor (4Z).

Varga: Leader of an Ice Warrior expedition sent to explore Earth in prehistoric times. He was found frozen in ice around AD 3000 and was freed by the Doctor. He later perished in the explosion of his own ship (OO).

Varlik: Warrior of the SWAMPIES. He became their leader after RANQUIN's death (5E).

Varsh: Alzarian OUTLER and brother of ADRIC. He was killed when the marshmen attacked the STAR-LINER (5R).

Vaughn (Tobias): Head of INTERNATIONAL ELECTROMATICS. He allied himself with the CYBERMEN and then helped the Doctor to destroy them (VV).

Vegetable Life: The Doctor encountered various types of vegetable life forms: deadly seaweed which absorbed people (RR), Martian SEEDS which emitted a lethal fungus (XX), intelligent KRYNOIDS (or Krynoid pods) (4L) and—worst of them all—MEGLOS, the cactus-like survivors of the Zolfa-Thurans (5Q). The planet CHLORIS's entire life and economy revolved around plant life, and so did that of the planet TYTHONUS (5G). The planet TIGELLA's vegetation was so aggressive that it drove the Tigellans underground (5Q).

Venusian Aiki-Do: The Doctor is one of the rare two-armed people who have mastered that art.

Vicki: One of the Doctor's companions. Ship-wrecked on the planet DIDO, she was rescued by the Doctor from the evil BENNETT. She left the Time Lord to marry Troilus (L–U).

Villar: Mexican revolutionary, he was a victim of the War Lords (ZZ).

Vira: Member of the space ARK, she fought against the WIRRN at the Doctor's side. After NOAH was taken over by the aliens, she became leader of the Ark (4C).

Virus: See NUCLEUS (4T) (Also BBB, XXX, 4D, 4J).

Vishinsky: Second in command of the Morestran expedition to ZETA MINOR. He replaced SALAMAR (4H).

Visians: Invisible hostile inhabitants of planet MIRA (V).

Visualiser (Time/Space): The First Doctor was given one by the Xerons for freeing the Space Museum (Q). It enabled him to see almost any scene in Time and Space (R).

Voga: Planet of Gold. The CYBERMEN destroyed it during the galactic Cyberwars. The last Vogans remained hidden inside the remains of their planet till one of their generals, VORUS, managed to attract the remaining Cybermen to space station NERVA (which was in orbit around Voga) and blow them up (4D).

Voords: Inhabitants of MARINUS. Their leader was YARTEK (E).

Vorg: Galactic showman and owner of the SCOPE which captured the TARDIS on INTER MINOR (PPP).

Vortis: Planet of the MENOPTERA and the ZARBI (N).

Vorus: Vogan general whose missile destroyed the CYBERMEN. His plans had been fiercely opposed by MAGRIK. Vorus died launching the missile which was to free his people (4D).

Vraxoin: Most dangerous and addictive drug in the Cosmos. It was smuggled by TRYST out of EDEN and onto the *Empress*. The Doctor discovered that it was made of the very substance of the Mandrels (5K).

Vulcan: Very distant Earth colony. It tried to use the DALEKS and ended having to fight them (EE).

Vynda-K (Graff): Deposed ruler of planet Levithia, he pursued the Doctor and GARRON on RIBOS—which he tried to buy! He died in an explosion of his own making (5A).

Vyon (Bret): Space Security Agent, he fought the DALEKS with the First Doctor and was killed trying to save the Time Lord. He was the brother of Sara KINGDOM (V).

Walker: He witnessed the destruction of the SEA DEVILS after having aborted peace attempts of the Doctor (LLL).

War Chief: Renegade Time Lord, he gave the SIDRATs to the WAR LORD's people. He was killed by the War Lord (ZZ).

Warlock (Dr): Friend of Professor SCARMAN, he was killed by SUTEKH (4G).

War Lord: Using stolen Time Lord technology, handed to them by the WAR CHIEF, the War Lord and his people recreated all of Earth's wars, with the aim of forming an army of invincible soldiers from the survivors. The Doctor put an end to their plans to conquer the Galaxy. The War Lord was tried and executed by the TIME LORDS (ZZ).

Watcher: Mysterious silhouette who followed and helped the Doctor in the LOGOPOLIS crisis. The Doctor's future self (5V).

Waterfield (Professor Edward and Victoria): Professor Waterfield was a 19th-century scientist who devised a time travel method involving mirrors and static electricity. He and his colleague Theodore MAXTIBLE attracted the DALEKS' attention, who used them, and the young Victoria Waterfield, to trap the Time Lord. Professor Waterfield was eventually killed by the Daleks. His daughter became one of the Doctor's companions. She eventually left him to remain on Earth in the 20th century (LL–RR).

Watkins (Professor and Isobel): Professor Watkins was a friend of the Doctor and of Professor TRAVERS. He and his niece, Isobel, helped the Time Lord to defeat the CYBERMEN invasion (VV).

Watson (Professor): Head of the nuclear research centre destroyed by ELDRAD (4N).

Weed: Creature from the sea which attacked men and turned them into weed-like beings. It attacked a refinery managed by ROBSON and was defeated by the Doctor after he found that high-frequency sound waves could kill it (RR).

Weng-Chiang: Chinese god. In reality a criminal from the future named Magnus GREEL (4S).

Wenley Moor: Location of a secret atomic research centre in Derbyshire, which also happened to be situated over a Silurian cave (BBB).

Wheel in Space: Space station invaded by CYBER-MATS and attacked by the CYBERMEN. It was saved by the Second Doctor and ZOE (SS).

Whitaker (Professor): Inventor of the TIME SCOOP which was to return Earth to its prehistoric past in OPERATION GOLDEN AGE. He and Charles GROVER were the victims of their plans (WWW).

Williams: General in charge of Earth's defence against the DRACONIANS (QQQ).

Winters (Miss): Leader of THINK TANK, she attempted to start the Third World War and used Professor KETTLEWELL's Giant Robot for her plans of world domination (4A).

Wirrn: Giant wasp-like aliens which travel though Space and breed on planets. Chased away from their own worlds by the Earth imperial expansion they took over space station NERVA and attempted to take over the bodies of the Humans. The leader of the ARK, NOAH, sacrificed himself to destroy them (4C).

Wolf Weeds: Carnivorous tumbleweeds from CHLORIS. They were used as weapons under the control of the HUNTSMAN (5G).

World Ecology Bureau: International organisation which allied itself with the Doctor in the Krynoid case (4L).

Wotan: Acronym for Will Operating Thought Analogue, a sentient super-computer built by Professor Brett at the top of the Post Office Tower. It built the War Machines and controlled telecommunications. It was destroyed by one of its own War Machines, reprogrammed by the First Doctor (BB).

Wright (Barbara): History teacher at COAL HILL SCHOOL. With her colleague Ian CHESTERTON, she followed SUSAN home and became one of the Doctor's companions (A–R).

Xanxia: Evil Queen of ZANAK and true mistress of the pirate planet. She needed the energies of entire worlds to keep her wizened form from aging and dying. She was killed in the rebellion engineered by the Doctor

(5B).

Xeros: Location of the MOROKS' space museum. The Doctor helped the Xerons to revolt against the Moroks—and thus change the future (Q).

Xoanon: Giant computer repaired by the Doctor. It acquired a double personality (the Doctor's), and created a warped world, provoking eternal war between the TESHS and the SEVATEEM, embodiments of the virtues of the Mind and of the Body. The Doctor restored it to sanity (4Q).

Yartek: Leader of the VOORDS. He perished in the destruction of the CONSCIENCE (E).

Yates (Captain): UNIT Captain. He betrayed the Brigadier in the OPERATION GOLDEN AGE case, but redeemed himself in the Giant SPIDERS adventure (EEE, FFF, GGG, JJJ, KKK, OOO, TTT, WWW, ZZZ).

Yetaxa: One-time High Priest of the Aztecs. Barbara was mistaken for his reincarnation (F).

Yeti: The real Yeti are peaceful, shy creatures. The hostile Yeti encountered by the Doctor are in reality robots controlled by the GREAT INTELLIGENCE with a small silver sphere inside their chests. The robot Yeti are directed by means of smaller replicas of themselves. Under the Great Intelligence's control, they invaded London (NN, QQ).

Za: Caveman (A).

Zanak: Hollow planet equipped with jump engines by the CAPTAIN. It travels through the vortex and rematerialises around another world, which it bleeds of its minerals and energies. It was secretly ruled by its Queen, XANXIA. Its pirate career was stopped by the Doctor and the MENTIADS (5B).

Zarbi: Giant ants controlled by the ANIMUS; they fought the MENOPTERA on VORTIS but became

harmless after the destruction of the Animus by the
CELL DESTRUCTOR (N).

Zargo: Formerly known as Captain Miles Sharkey of
the Earth ship *Hydrax*. Drawn into E-SPACE by the
GREAT VAMPIRE, he became one of the immortal
vampire rulers of a local planet (along with AUKON
and CAMILLA). He died when the Doctor destroyed
the Great Vampire (5B).

Zaroff (Professor): Mad scientist who enslaved the
fishmen from ATLANTIS and was planning the
destruction of Earth by draining the ocean into its
molten core. He was the victim of his own plans (GG).

Zastor: Leader of TIGELLA. He sent for the Doctor
when the power of the DODECAHEDRON started to
fail (5Q).

Z-Bomb: A secret Earth weapon used in an abortive
attempt to destroy the CYBERMEN's home planet,
MONDAS (DD).

Zeos: Twin planet of ATRIOS, with which it was at
war. It appeared to be deserted but for the MENTALIS
Machine (5F).

Zeta Minor: Planet where a Morestran expedition led
by Professor Sorensen found ANTI-MATTER. It
contained a gate leading to another universe (4H).

Zigma Experiment: Flawed time travel experiment
devised by Magnus GREEL (4S).

Zoe: One of the Doctor's companions. She joined the
Time Lord on the WHEEL IN SPACE and eventually
was sent back to her own era by the TIME LORDS
(SS–ZZ).

Zolfa-Thura: Sister planet of TIGELLA. The Zolfa-
Thurans all died in a huge planetary war to prevent
MEGLOS from using the power of the DODECA-
HEDRON, magnified by the screens of Zolfa-Thura, to
ravage the Universe (5Q).

Zygons: Aliens who landed in Loch Ness centuries ago.
Their home planet was subsequently destroyed and

they prepared the invasion of Earth with the help of their shape-changing abilities and of their SKARASEN. Their leader, BROTON, his crew and spaceship were destroyed by UNIT (4F).

3 Who's Who on *Who*

ADAMS (Douglas): Script Editor 5J–5M; Writer 5B, 5H, with Graham WILLIAMS as David AGNEW 5M

AGNEW (David): Writer (household name used by other writers) 4Z, 5H

ASHBY (Norman): Writer TT

BAKER (Bob): Writer 5K; with Dave MARTIN GGG, NNN, RRR, 4B, 4N, 4T, 4Y, 5F

BARRY (Christopher): Director B, L, M, AA, EE, JJJ, NNN, 4A, 4K, 5G

BARRY (Morris): Director HH, MM, TT

BENNETT (Rodney): Director 4C, 4B, 4M

BERNARD (Paul): Director KKK, OOO, QQQ

BICKFORD (Lovett): Director 5N

BIDMEAD (Christopher H.): Script Editor 5N–5V; Writer 5V

BLACK (Ian Stuart): Writer AA, JJ, with Kit PEDLER and Pat DUNLAP BB

BLACK (John): Director 5T

BLAKE (Darrol): Director 5C

BLAKE (Gerald): Director NN, 4Z

BLAND (Robin): see DICKS (Terrance)

BOUCHER (Chris): Writer 4Q, 4R, 4X

BRIANT (Michael): Director HHH, LLL, TTT, XXX, 4D, 4R

BROMLY (Alan): Director UUU, 5K

BRYANT (Peter): Producer KK–MM, QQ–YY; Script Editor LL, NN–PP

BYRNE (Johnny): Writer 5T

CAMFIELD (Douglas): Director J, P, S, V, QQ, VV,
    DDD, 4F, 4L
COBURN (Anthony): Writer A
COMBE (Timothy): Director BBB, FFF
COTTON (Donald): Writer U, Z
COX (Frank): Director C, G
CROCKET (John): Director F

DAVID (Hugh): Director FF, RR
DAVIES (John): Director JJ
DAVIS (Gerry): Script Editor Y–LL; Writer 4D, with
    Kit PEDLER DD, MM, with Elwyn JONES FF;
    Book adaptations DD, MM
DICKS (Terrance): Script Editor VV–XX, ZZ–ZZZ;
    Writer 4A, 4V, 5P; under the name of Robin
    BLAND 4K, with Malcolm HULKE ZZ; Book
    adaptations K, NN, QQ, AAA, EEE, GGG,
    KKK, NNN, RRR, PPP, SSS, UUU, XXX,
    YYY, ZZZ, 4A, 4E, 4D, 4F, 4H, 4G, 4J, 4K, 4N,
    4P, 4Q, 4R, 4S, 4V, 4T, 4X, 4Y, 4Z, 5C, 5D, 5E,
    5F, 5J, 5K, 5L
DUDLEY (Terence): Director 5Q
DUNLAP (Pat): Writer, with Ian Stuart BLACK and
    Kit PEDLER BB

ELLIS (David): Writer, with Malcolm HULKE KK
EMMS (William): Writer T
ERICKSON (Paul): Writer, with Lesley SCOTT Y

FERGUSON (Michael): Director BB, XX, CCC, GGG
FISHER (David): Writer 5C, 5D, 5G, 5N; Book
    adaptation 5G
FLANAGAN (John): Writer, with Andrew
    McCULLOCH 5Q

GALLAGHER (Steve): Writer 5S

GOODWIN (Derrick): Director 4T
GORRIE (John): Director E
GRAINER (Ron): Composer of the *Doctor Who* theme
    music
GRIEVE (Ken): Director 5J
GRIMWADE (Peter): Director 5R, 5V

HAISMAN (Mervyn): Writer with Henry LINCOLN
    NN, QQ
HARRIS (STEPHEN): Writer 4G
HART (Michael): Director YY
HAYES (Michael): Director 5D, 5F, 5H
HAYLES (Brian): Writer X, CC, OO, XX, MMM,
    YYY; Book adaptations OO, MMM
HINCHCLIFFE (Philip): Producer 4C–4S; Book
    adaptation E, 4L, 4M
HIRSCH (Henrick): Director H
HOLMES (Robert): Script Editor 4A–4W; Writer
    WW, YY, AAA, EEE, PPP, UUU, 4C, 4P, 4S,
    4W, 5A, 5E
HOUGHTON (Don): Writer DDD, FFF
HULKE (Malcolm): Writer BBB, HHH, LLL, QQQ,
    WWW, with David ELLIS KK, with Terrance
    DICKS ZZ; Book adaptations ZZ, BBB, HHH,
    LLL, QQQ, TTT, WWW
HUSSEIN (Waris): Director A, D

IMISON (Michael): Director Y

JONES (Elwyn): Writer, with Gerry DAVIS FF
JONES (Glyn): Writer Q
JOYCE (Paul): Director 5S

LAMBERT (Verity): Producer A–T/A
LEOPOLD (Guy): Pseudonym for Barry LETTS
    writing with Robert SLOMAN JJJ
LESTON-SMITH (Michael): Director U

LETTS (Barry): Executive Producer 5N–5V; Producer
BBB–4A; Director PP, EEE, PPP, ZZZ, 4J;
Writer, with Robert SLOMAN as Guy
LEOPOLD JJJ; Book adaptation JJJ
LINCOLN (Henry): Writer, with Mervyn HAISMAN
NN, QQ
LING (Peter): Writer UU
LLOYD (Innes): Producer X–LL, NN–PP
LUCAROTTI (John): Writer D, F, W

McBAIN (Kenny): Director 5L
MALONEY (David): Director UU, WW, ZZ, SSS,
4E, 4H, 4P, 4S
MARKS (Louis): Writer J, KKK, 4H, 4M
MARTER (Ian): Book adaptations 4C, 4B, 5A
MARTIN (Dave): Writer, with Bob BAKER GGG,
NNN, RRR, 4B, 4N, 4T, 4Y, 5F
MARTIN (Richard): Director C, K, N, R
MARTINUS (Derek): Director T, T/A, DD, LL, OO,
AAA
MAYNE (Lennie): Director MMM, RRR, YYY, 4N
McCULLOCH (Andrew): Writer, with John
FLANAGAN 5Q
MILL (Gerry): Director KK
MOFFATT (Peter): Director 5P

NATHAN-TURNER (John): Producer 5N–5V
NATION (Terry): Writer B, E, K, R, T/A, V, SSS,
XXX, 4E, 4J, 5J
NEWMAN (Peter): Writer G

ORME (Geoffrey): Writer GG

PEDLER (Kit): Writer HH, with Ian Stuart BLACK
and Pat DUNLAP BB, with Gerry DAVIS DD,
MM, with David WHITAKER SS, with Derrick
SHERWIN VV

PEMBERTON (Victor): Script Editor MM; Writer RR
PINFIELD (Mervyn): Producer A–M; Director G, J, Q

READ (Anthony): Script Editor 4Y–5F; Writer 5L
ROBERTS (Pennant): Director 4Q, 4W, 5B, 5M
RUSSELL (Paddy): Director W, WWW, 4G, 4V

SCOTT (Lesley): Writer, with Paul ERICKSON Y
SELLARS (Bill): Director X
SHERWIN (Derrick): Producer ZZ–AAA; Script
    Editor QQ–UU, YY; Writer, with Kit PEDLER
    VV
SIMPSON (Dudley): Incidental Music
SLOMAN (Robert): Writer OOO, TTT, ZZZ, with
    Barry LETTS as Guy LEOPOLD JJJ
SMITH (Andrew): Writer 5R
SMITH (Julia): Director CC, GG
SPENTON-FOSTER (George): Director 4X, 5A
SPOONER (Dennis): Script Editor L–R; Writer H,
    M, S, V
STEWART (Norman): Director 4Y, 5E
STEWART (Robert Banks): Writer 4F, 4L
STRUTTON (Bill): Writer N; Book adaptation N

TOSH (Donald): Script Editor S–W
TUCKER (Rex): Director Z
de VERE COLE (Tristan): Director SS

WHITAKER (David): Script Editor A–K; Writer C,
    L, P, EE, LL, PP, CCC, with Kit PEDLER SS;
    Book adaptation: A/B, P
WILES (John): Producer U–Y
WILLIAMS (Graham): Producer 4V–5M; Writer,
    with Douglas ADAMS as David AGNEW 5H

4 Book Adaptations

First Doctor

A/B	David Whitaker
E	Philip Hinchcliffe
K	Terrance Dicks
N	Bill Strutton
P	David Whitaker
DD	Gerry Davis

Second Doctor

HH	Gerry Davis
MM	Gerry Davis
NN	Terrance Dicks
OO	Brian Hayles
QQ	Terrance Dicks
ZZ	Malcolm Hulke

Third Doctor

AAA	Terrance Dicks
BBB	Malcolm Hulke
EEE	Terrance Dicks
GGG	Terrance Dicks
HHH	Malcolm Hulke
JJJ	Barry Letts
KKK	Terrance Dicks
MMM	Brian Hayles
LLL	Malcolm Hulke
NNN	Terrance Dicks
RRR	Terrance Dicks
PPP	Terrance Dicks

QQQ	Malcolm Hulke
SSS	Terrance Dicks
TTT	Malcolm Hulke
UUU	Terrance Dicks
WWW	Malcolm Hulke
XXX	Terrance Dicks
YYY	Terrance Dicks
ZZZ	Terrance Dicks

Fourth Doctor

4A	Terrance Dicks
4C	Ian Marter
4B	Ian Marter
4E	Terrance Dicks
4D	Terrance Dicks
4F	Terrance Dicks
4H	Terrance Dicks
4G	Terrance Dicks
4J	Terrance Dicks
4K	Terrance Dicks
4L	Philip Hinchcliffe
4M	Philip Hinchcliffe
4N	Terrance Dicks
4P	Terrance Dicks
4Q	Terrance Dicks
4R	Terrance Dicks
4S	Terrance Dicks
4V	Terrance Dicks
4T	Terrance Dicks

4X	Terrance Dicks
4Y	Terrance Dicks
4Z	Terrance Dicks
5A	Ian Marter
5C	Terrance Dicks
5D	Terrance Dicks
5E	Terrance Dicks
5F	Terrance Dicks
5G	David Fisher
5J	Terrance Dicks
5K	Terrance Dicks
5L	Terrance Dicks

APPENDICES

The following uses of the *Doctor Who* character and concepts are not technically part of the 'Whoniverse' and therefore have not been included in the previous indexes. They are listed here for reference only.

1 The Films

Doctor Who and the Daleks (1965)
Executive Producer: Joe Vegoda
Producers: Milton Subotsky and Max J. Rosenberg
Director: Gordon Flemyng
Screenplay: Milton Subotsky

Regal Films and Lion International
Cast: Peter Cushing (Dr Who); Roy Castle (Ian Chesterton); Jennie Linden (Barbara); Roberta Tovey (Susan); Barrie Ingham, Geoffrey Toone, Mark Petersen, John Brown, Michael Coles, Yvonne Antrobus.

Based on Terry Nation's story (B)

The Daleks: Invasion Earth 2150 AD (1966)
Executive Producer: Joe Vegoda
Producers: Milton Subotsky and Max J. Rosenberg
Director: Gordon Flemyng
Screenplay: Milton Subotsky

Lion International
Cast: Peter Cushing (Dr Who); Bernard Cribbins (Tom Campbell); Ray Brooks (David); Andrew Keir (Wyler); Keith Marsh (Conway); Jill Curzon (Louise); Roberta Tovey (Susan); Roger Avon (Wells); Steve Peters, Philip Madoc, Eddie Powell, Godfrey Quigley, Tony Reynolds, Bernard Spear, Sheila Steafel, Eileen Way, Kenneth Watson, John Wreford, Robert Jewell.
Special Effects: Ted Samuels
Music: Bill McGuffie

Based on Terry Nation's story (K)

In these films the Doctor is called Doctor Who. He is not a Time Lord but a scientist from Earth who has invented a TARDIS. He has two granddaughters, and Susan is only 9 years old in the film version.

2 The Stage Play

Doctor Who and the Daleks in Seven Keys to Doomsday (1974)
Adelphi Theatre, London, 4 weeks from 16 December
1974

Written by: Terrance Dicks
Designed by: John Napier
Directed by: Mick Hughes
Sound: Philip Clifford
Production Supervisor: Trevor Mitchell
Production Coordinator for the BBC: Barry Letts
Fight Arranging: Mo Kiki
Monster Coordination: James Acheson
Cast: Trevor Martin (the Doctor); Wendy Padbury
(Jenny); James Mathews (Jimmy); Ian Ruskin (Jedak);
Patsy Dermott (Tara); Anthony Garner (Garm); Simon
Jones (Master of Karn); Jacquie Dubin (Dalek
Emperor); Robin Browne (Marco); Peter Jolley, Mo
Kiki, Peter Whitting (Clawrentulars); Peter Jolley
(Dalek dialogue).
Story: The Doctor and his two companions, Jenny and
Jimmy, prevent the Daleks and their crab-like slaves, the
Clawrentulars, finding the seven crystals of Karn which
would enable them to control all life in the Universe.

Originally planned for Jon Pertwee, the Doctor's role
was taken by Trevor Martin, whilst Wendy Padbury
(Zoe in the TV series) played one of his companions.
Opening scenes showed a screen with the face of Pertwee
changing into Martin's. Some of the concepts—the

Planet Karn, the psychic battle between the Doctor and the Master of Karn, etc.—were later used by Terrance Dicks in his story *The Brain of Morbius* (4K).

3 The Records

Doctor Who Theme Music (1964) BBC
Doctor Who and the Daleks (1965) Century 21
Who is Doctor Who (1968) BBC
Who is the Doctor (1972) EMI
Doctor Who and the Pescatons (1976) DECCA
Doctor Who Sound Effects (1978) BBC
Doctor Who—Mankind (1979) Pinnacle
Doctor Who and the Genesis of the Daleks (1979) BBC
Doctor Who Theme Music (1980) BBC